THE JOLLY ROGER
PIRATE RADIO DAYS IN CORK

Trevor & Noel Welch
with Ralph Riegel

The Jolly Roger
Pirate Radio Days in Cork

CURRACH PRESS

First published in 2015 by Currach Press
55A Spruce Avenue
Stillorgan Industrial Park
Blackrock
Co. Dublin
Ireland
www.currach.ie

ISBN: 978 1 78218 847 6

The poem on the back cover appears courtesy
of Lilian O'Donoghue, née McCarthy

Book design by Helene Pertl | Currach Press
Printed by Scandbook

This book is dedicated to the memory of Henry Condon –
an original Cork pirate, an accomplished radio pioneer
and a great friend.

ACKNOWLEDGEMENTS

This book began as a dream almost ten years ago. We are deeply indebted to a number of people for helping us to defy the odds and finally bring that dream to fruition.

Firstly, to Patrick O'Donoghue and his team at Currach Press for having the faith, and no little courage, to support this project.

Secondly, to Ralph Riegel of *The Irish Independent* for his hard work and patience in transforming the tapes into a manuscript.

Thirdly, to our generous sponsors – Brian Lennox, Denis 'Dino' Cregan, Liam Ryan of Togher SuperValu and Conal Thomas of Conal's Tree Services – without whose support this might very well have remained a great idea rather than the book you hold in your hands.

An enormous amount of work went into this project and it was supported every step of the way by our families. So special thanks to Trevor's partner Gillian Greene, Sarah and Jack, his mum, Eileen Welch, dad, Noel Welch Snr and sisters, Janet, Valerie, Sharon, Hazel, Avril and Eileen.

Thanks also to Noel's wife Dolores, sons and daughters David, Kevin, Susan and Caroline and his four grandchildren, Kian, Amy, Zac and Emily.

Interviews for this book took place over five years and we are very grateful to those who agreed to speak of their experiences, both good and bad, of pirate radio and to raid old scrapbooks and memory stores about those heady days in Cork in the 1970s and 1980s. If you get half the joy from reading this book that we got from researching and writing it, the entire project will have been very worthwhile.

So thanks to: Shay Curran, Jack Lyons, Michael Corcoran, Jim Collins, Peter O'Neill, PJ Cassidy, Dan Noonan, Barry O'Mahony, Eric Faldo, Henry Condon, Neil Prendeville, Ken Tobin, Rob Allen, PJ Coogan, Pat McAuliffe, Matthew McAuliffe, Paul Byrne, Romano Macari, John Creedon, Steve Bolger, Gerry Newman, Pierce McCarthy, Michael Lynam, Fergal Barry, Mark Cagney, Nick Richards, Lilian O'Donoghue, née McCarthy, John Greene, Michael O'Sullivan, Ian Richards, Ken Regis, Colin Noone, Brian Gunn, Bob Stokes, Brendan McCarthy, Eddie O'Hare, John Patrick, Tony Whitnell, Pat Egan, Tony Magnier, Derry O'Callaghan, Don Walsh, Phillip Johnston, John Ger O'Riordan, Patricia Deeney, Stephen Grainger, Colm Moore and Dominic Murphy.

Ralph would particularly like to thank Newstalk's Jonathan Healy – representing the latest wave of Cork radio stars – for his valuable input and advice on the manuscript. Thanks also to TV3's Paul Byrne for his humour, great stories and friendship.

Trevor Welch, Noel Welch and Ralph Riegel

FOREWORD

Pat Egan, record store owner and concert promoter: 'Looking back, I can see why people consider the 1970s and 1980s to be a golden period in Cork, particularly for music. To be honest, I can't think about that period in Cork and the pirate radio stations and the gigs without thinking of Rory Gallagher. Viewing it now from a distance of over forty years I can say that they were amongst the best years of my life.

'I love Cork – I always have. I still keep an involvement in the city and, even now, I am running gigs in Cork Opera House. So much has been done to improve the city and transform the city centre. It is a terrific place but has still managed to keep that friendliness and warmth that I always liked about it.

'But Cork people are still as tight with their money as ever – when we sold stuff from the record shops we had to have a bargain section. Albums used to fly from that section because Cork people always loved a bargain.

'Before I opened my record stores in Cork, I was in the city writing the group scene or the "Beat Pages", as they were called, for *Spotlight* magazine. The magazine at the time was ninety per cent showbands and the other types of groups were really just an afterthought. My main memory was going down for various gigs in City Hall where I worked as a DJ. I was there for Thin Lizzy, or rather Skid Row because Lizzy came later. I also spent time in the Savoy. But it was mostly City Hall and later working there with Rory. Other than Rory and Taste, Sleepy Hollow was the other main band that I remember from that era.

'I ran the Sound Cellar record store in Dublin, which was the first of its kind. It was in an underground cellar just off Grafton Street and it became a kind of institution. Dave Fanning used to say that the only place where you could get albums in the 1970s, at roughly the same time as they were launched in the UK, was Sound Cellar. I realised that stuff was arriving into Ireland five or six weeks after the UK launches. So I started to source stuff directly and that helped us a lot. There were a huge amount of fans here but they just couldn't get the records. It seems incredible now looking back on it.

'The Sound Cellar was very successful and then I opened another shop on Duke Street. Oliver Barry, a Corkman who was in the showband business, told me I should open up in Cork. He loaned me IR£500 and we set up a shop at 20 Patrick Street. We took a lease and, at the time, there was only Ursula's Record Store and UNEEDA Books selling records. We were pretty trendy in Cork.

'I had great customers, like Mark Cagney who was into all the early releases. Stevie Bolger, who is a friend of mine to this day, was another great customer. I suppose it is only now that I look back and realise just what a special time that was for the people I dealt with and the friends I made.

'Then we opened record stores in the Savoy Arcade and opened on Princes Street and later the Queen's Old Castle. We had four shops in Cork at our peak but, as the recession of the 1980s came in, business fell off. I split up with Oliver at that stage and we were lucky that we had purchased the premises on Patrick Street so we got a return on our investment.

'I lived at 120 Patrick Street at the time up on the third floor. I was there for about five years or more and my front window looked right down onto Patrick Street. I saw some sights there over the years – people being dragged along the street and, in one case, a guy with an axe running across the street after a fella. There was another guy who drove a big cattle truck and he would park it full of cattle or sheep on the street directly outside my window at night while he disappeared into one of the nightclubs.

'I decided to keep one shop in the Queen's Old Castle arcade for a number of years but my general memories of Cork all relate to Rory Gallagher, one way or another. I had a good relationship with Rory and his brother, Donal. I would either travel down to Cork with them in the car or they came with me. I was often up in the house in Douglas with them.

'I can say now, with the benefit of hindsight, that Rory's gigs in City Hall were probably the standout gigs in Cork, if not Ireland, from that period. And that is judging him in some very fine company. I went to Cork with Fleetwood Mac when they were at the very top of their game. It was a really terrific time to be into music in Cork. I never realised at the time that we were all effectively becoming part of the history of popular music.

'The Savoy was another terrific venue. I know Cork is considering a new concert venue, and of course you have Peter Aiken running 'Live at the Marquee', which is a great music series. But the Savoy and City Hall were great venues, and yet, every time I recall them, all I can think of is Rory. He was such a gentle, gentle man but such an enormous talent – it was a real pleasure to be mates with him. My fondest memories of Cork are the record shops and spending time with Rory – how could that not be a standout memory?

'It is a little sad today that you look around and don't see bands like Taste on the scene. There were so many great bands back then. I ran a lot of gigs in City Hall in my early days. I ran Van Morrison, Eric Clapton, Status Quo – they were days when we could get 3,000 people into City Hall. It was a good bit before even U2 played that venue. I was there that night and I remember meeting Larry Mullen in the old Jury's Hotel – he was the only guy in U2 that I would have a nodding relationship with. But I did give U2 one of their first ever big gigs when I booked them with The Stranglers for the Top Hat in Dublin. We paid them IR£50 for the gig. It's crazy looking back on it now.

'The whole pirate radio thing was part and parcel of what was going on in the music industry back then. Mike Hogan, who was involved with Radio Nova in Dublin pulled me into a lot of stuff that was going on – things like promotional gigs and the like. There was a lad who used to work in the shop in Cork for us called Michael Murphy and he is now involved in film production.

'You can see now, with the wisdom of forty years looking back, that the young DJs on the pirate radio stations were really ahead of the game. They were like the young lads in the IT industry who score big with the tech start-ups. They knew what was going on in terms of music development and knew what people wanted to listen to. That's why you had really good guys like Mark Cagney, Stevie Bolger and others haunting our record shops for the latest releases.

'It's hard to credit but, with RTÉ back then, you didn't hear Rory Gallagher or Van Morrison or any of those great guys. They just weren't played on RTÉ. That's why the pirates were so successful when they came on the scene – they were giving people the music they wanted to listen to.

'The 1960s, to be fair, was where it all began in music terms. But for the development of Irish bands it was all about the 1970s. The sad thing today is that a lot of the creative element has gone from music. A lot of it is stuff that is simply churned out for commercial purposes. But who am I to judge young people and what they listen to today? I just think we were very lucky in that period to have Van Morrison, Rory Gallagher, Phil Lynott and then The Boomtown Rats and U2. I knew Phil well before Thin Lizzy had the hit with "Whiskey In The Jar". The point is that there were tons of great acts on the scene – it was a terrific period to be involved in music.

'Was it Ireland's golden period for music? It certainly was for us. But what made it so special was the characters involved in the scene and the fun we all had together. I suppose one way of judging it is that, all these years later, we are still talking about gigs that happened in City Hall, the Savoy and the Arcadia. The music was terrific. But just imagine the magic of being able to call Rory Gallagher a mate!'

CONTENTS

INTRODUCTION

It was a time of magic. When, for a single glorious decade, imagination triumphed over commercial reality. Pirate radio station DJs compiled playlists based purely on their love for the music; broadcast studios were in old caravans and even rat-infested farmyards; stars adopted exotic-sounding names to woo listeners; outside broadcast units were invariably the back seats of old Ford Cortinas or Opel Asconas and every DJ lived in mortal terror that the Gardaí might arrive to shut their station down or, worse still, confiscate their precious private record collections.

Pirate radio wasn't a Cork phenomenon. It first emerged in Dublin in the 1970s before exploding in popularity in the early 1980s. But pirate radio was adopted with such a passion in Cork that, three decades later, stations like ERI, SouthCoast, CBC, ABC, Radio Caroline, WBEN, CCLR, Capitol Radio, NCLR and others are remembered with a fondness far beyond mere nostalgia.

In Cork, pirate radio stations gave voice to a city that felt itself both forgotten and beleaguered. It introduced generations of youngsters to music that, until the emergence of 2FM, would never have been played on RTÉ Radio 1.

An old caravan in Togher became a rival for Radio Luxembourg, Capitol Radio's upstairs studio on Tuckey Street became a mecca for Cork schoolchildren and a cow barn off

Dublin Hill served for a time as a broadcasting headquarters when SouthCoast was raided.

The very imagination and exuberance of the pirates provided a form of escapism for a city struggling to adapt to the realities of modern Ireland. In 1984, arguably the high watermark for Cork pirate radio stations, the city was left economically on its knees as first Dunlop and then Ford closed major manufacturing plants. Almost 2,000 jobs were lost in those two Marina plants alone and the writing was on the wall for other old Cork industries including, Sunbeam, Verolme Dockyard, Irish Steel and Thompsons. Unemployment soared to over twenty per cent in some areas. For some, the only escape from the grim local industrial reality was the records they listened to in their bedrooms and the pirate radio stations they loyally tuned into each evening.

There was no talk of Donnybrook, O'Connell Street, Ballsbridge or Grafton Street. It was Cork news for Cork people – and listeners switched their radio dials by the thousands for traffic reports from St Luke's and the Lower Glanmire Road, shopping updates from Patrick Street and Oliver Plunkett Street and news of Mary Murphy's missing Jack Russell from Blarney Street.

Such was the popularity of the pirate stations that they launched the careers of some of Ireland's best-loved broadcasters today: John Creedon, Neil Prendeville, Paul Byrne, Ken Tobin, PJ Coogan, Trevor Welch, Mark Cagney, Michael Corcoran, Stevie Bolger and a galaxy of others.

CCLR founder, Shay Curran, puts it best as he argued that, if you weren't going to be a football or GAA star and if you weren't in a rock band, being a DJ on an Irish pirate radio station in the 1970s and 1980s was about as cool as it ever got.

Most operated under exotic-sounding aliases. Some began their broadcasting careers while they were still preparing for their Leaving Cert exams. The majority worked for free and ultimately made their living through playing DJ at some of Cork's booming disco clubs including, Chandras, De Lacy House, Coco's and Zoe's. A week of broadcasting sometimes resulted in an IR£10 note on a Friday evening which was usually spent on a few drinks, a snooker session and burgers and chips with other 'jocks'.

Stations came and went depending on the finances of their owners and the mood of Cork youth. There was CBC, NCLR, Radio Caroline, WBEN, ERI, SouthCoast, Capitol Radio and a dozen others. The innocence of the early pirates was slowly replaced by the commercial realisation of the latter era 'super pirates' such as ERI and SouthCoast. Both recognised that audiences were there to be won from RTÉ and, to do so properly, required investment in both decent studios and equipment. Most of all, they got a glimpse of the future in that commercial radio was potentially a money-making machine.

Ultimately, it was the very success of SouthCoast and ERI that spelled the end for the pirate radio era. The government, after a fifteen-year debate with RTÉ about precisely what to do, issued licenses for local radio stations in 1989 following a bitterly contested selection process.

Pirate stations, desperate for a chance to go legitimate, carefully complied with new broadcasting rules lest they foil their chances of gaining one of the prized licenses. The government, for its part, was determined to get rid of the old pirates and start profiting from the taxes to be paid by their legitimate and strictly licensed successors.

The predictions of doom from RTÉ and provincial

newspaper owners failed to materialise and, within a few years, the newly licensed local radio stations were as much a part of the fabric of new Irish society as Radio Éireann ever was in 'old Ireland'. From a position where newspaper and RTÉ journalists, all members of the National Union of Journalists (NUJ), would walk out of press conferences if a non-unionised pirate radio reporter arrived, radio reporters with licensed stations flocked to join the union and, within a few years, became stalwarts of the NUJ.

But the new stations, despite their pirate roots, never quite managed to recapture the excitement, whiff of danger, spark of imagination or anti-authoritarianism that their predecessors so effortlessly created in their pirate heyday. Increased profits brought greater professionalism, market surveys, playlists, audience research and 'radio doctors' from Dublin and London to help programmes better target market share.

Commercial success ultimately holed the pirate radio ship well below the waterline. But it didn't sink without trace. The careers pirate radio launched continue to flourish on Ireland's airways and those DJs never forgot their roots or the magic of that special time in the late 1970s and early 1980s. To this day, most DJs admit that their favourite time in radio was on the old pirate stations.

The Cork stars who owed their first big break to those pirate outfits still pay tribute to the stations involved in an era of *Dallas*-style hairdos, flared trousers, denim jackets, Ford Capris and Opel Mantas, disco music, twenty-four-hour snooker marathons, all-conquering Rebel GAA teams and Cork's bid to wrestle the title of entertainment capital away from Dublin.

For Cork's pirate radio stars, for an all too brief time in the 1980s, anything seemed possible. This is their story.

CHAPTER ONE

The bulk of the uniformed figure in the studio doorway immediately caught the young DJ's attention. Every pirate radio station lived in mortal fear of An Garda Síochána in the 1970s and 1980s. Pirate radio station DJs had a particular terror and it revolved around losing their precious personal record collections to an over-zealous garda with no guarantee it would ever be returned after a Department of Posts and Telegraphs authorised raid.

'There was no such thing as a station record archive. You brought your own records with you and if you lost them or had them taken, you were up the creek without a paddle,' 96FM's talk show anchor, PJ Coogan, recalled from his Radio Caroline and SouthCoast Radio days.

That summer day in the early 1980s, PJ was live on air with SouthCoast when he spotted the figure looming in the doorway. The broadcaster was well able to recognise an officer of the law, given that his father was a retired sergeant based in Carrigaline. He presumed it was a raid and that studio equipment – including his own record collection – was now at serious risk.

'He looked at me and asked if there was any chance I could play a request for the Gardaí that were out on patrol in Cork? I couldn't believe it. I was shocked. I said there was absolutely no problem and promised that I'd dedicate the very next record

5

to them. I was in shock but curiosity eventually got the better of me and, as he turned to walk away, I asked him why the Gardaí tuned in to us when they could be listening to RTÉ?

'He turned back to look at me and said: "We don't have much choice." He took out his garda radio and when he clicked the transmit button all you could hear coming over the receiver was SouthCoast. I think the song that was being played was Eddie Rabbitt's "I Love a Rainy Night". I'd say he was telling stories in the station for weeks afterwards about the look on my face.'

Few realised it but the mid 1980s was both the golden era of pirate radio in Cork and its swansong. By 1989, all the pirate stations would close, some with one eye on clinching one of the prized Independent Radio Television Commission (IRTC) licenses that would, as many correctly predicted, effectively become licenses to print money in years to come.

In Cork, pirate radio stations would become such professional outfits and with such resources that they became dubbed 'super pirates'. Stations such as ERI and SouthCoast in the 1980s were as professional as RTÉ, but with the advantage of having a major spirit of adventure. Yet they were a far cry from the early Cork pirates who broadcast from bedsits off St Patrick's Hill and Middle Glanmire Road, and whose studio equipment was little more than a boosted DJ disco deck.

But Cork's pirate radio story goes farther back than the 1970s. In 1964, a group of Cork schoolboys were so taken by Radio Luxembourg and Radio Caroline they decided to try and emulate them. The result was Radio Juliet which, while it only lasted for a matter of weeks, ranks as Cork's first official pirate radio station. The station was broadcast thanks to bits of leftover electrical equipment coupled with huge schoolboy ingenuity. But its range was less than a mile and its existence passed most people in Cork by.

Annmarie McIntyre's academic study of the subculture of pirate radio in Cork revealed that the station was set up by schoolboys who invested the princely sum of six shillings for the equipment they needed. This enabled them to get the gear, most of it cast-offs, to construct their own homemade transmitter, with an aerial being manufactured from some salvaged wire and metal poles.

'They had their own records and enough brass neck to take the music they loved to the airwaves, if only for a short time,' she wrote. But if Radio Juliet didn't have longevity, at least it fired the imagination of young people across Cork, who were increasingly conscious of the fact the music they loved simply wasn't being played by RTÉ.

In 1971, another pirate radio station made its debut. It was the brainchild of the late Jack O'Regan, who adored the latest wave of UK bands including Pink Floyd, Led Zeppelin and Marc Bolan and T. Rex. Appropriately enough, it later came to become known as Radio Cobweb.

Jack set up his transmitter in the garden shed of his Glasheen family home and, with the able support of his brother, Joe, devoted broadcasts to bands which never had a hope of appearing on Radio Éireann. Again, transmission power was a major issue from the shed with the station's range usually less than two miles. Local youths, awestruck by the O'Regan brothers and their commitment to music, dubbed the radio shed the 'Bunk House'.

Jack died in July 1998 and a tribute in *The Cork Examiner* was fulsome in its praise of the adventurous spirit he brought to the local arts world: 'From his early teens to the period prior to his death, he was a ceaseless exponent of radio broadcasting, measured in testimony by his vast knowledge of contemporary rock music and a long-standing appreciation of blues legend Rory Gallagher.

'Jack O'Regan is (now) folklore and has been for as long as most of us can remember. He will be fondly remembered by his many friends in the music fraternity and beyond, as the original pirate radio broadcaster. O'Regan brought a breath of freshness and originality with his zany radio shows when he began broadcasting in 1971 from his family back garden shed.

'Nobody had ever heard of Radio Cobweb when it first hit the pirate airwaves but soon it was the talk of Cork's pop pickers. A further O'Regan initiative was Radio Skywave.

'In many ways, Jack was a forerunner of things to come. Accompanied by his unassuming brother Joe in most of his exploits, he was the first (and only) person to record a live gig by Rory Gallagher's band 'Taste' at Cork's Cavern Club on Easter Sunday 1967.

'Later, in 1972, the O'Regan brothers filmed Gallagher in concert at the City Hall. To this day, both the highly collectable Cavern recording and City Hall film have been preserved in faithful storage by the Glasheen rocker. Jack (later) began to suffer the toll of what sadly turned out to be an incurable illness. Yet, despite great pain and obvious discomfort, he was instrumental in the presentation of a public talk on the subject of pirate radio and Gallagher at the Triskel Arts Centre.

'To his credit, he was able to entertain an appreciative audience with memorabilia that included sound recordings from his radio shows, film footage and rare press cuttings. As one would have expected, the talk concluded with a standing ovation.'

Jack Lyons, a postal worker who achieved legendary status in Cork through his friendship with The Who during his London days, became a huge fan. 'I think pirate radio was almost an essential part of growing up in Cork. To be honest, I actually think some of the stations were better when they were pirates than when they later became legitimate.

'Jack O'Regan was one of the early pioneers. You could hear anything with him. He would play everything from The Rolling Stones right up to Frank Zappa. Sometimes his signal would come through on the band for RTÉ TV. Looking back on it now, it was the very start of the pirate radio revolution.

'It was a funny time. Take the Rolling Stones – they were the very people that fathers told their daughters to stay away from, both for their music and the crowd that followed them. Pirate radio was a bit like that. In many ways, pirate radio in Cork was like listening to Radio Luxembourg. The pirates had a certain mystique about them similar to bands like the Rolling Stones, The Who and some of the American bands. It was radio without a licence and you got a sense it was in the spirit of what rock 'n' roll was all about. It was not so much illegal as it was rebellious.'

Jack admitted that the early Cork pirates were far from professional and simply getting a signal to tune in to was a challenge. 'There were some very colourful characters involved. No one was radio trained, their voices were all over the place and you could hear almost anything on the air. But it didn't matter. People could come out with anything, for instance, a lad who left an album on the No. 10 bus called in and asked if someone could check at the Bus Éireann hut on Patrick Street to see if a conductor had handed it in?'

Jack went on to become a huge fan of SouthCoast, while his wife was a major supporter of ERI. One of his fondest memories was listening to John Creedon, aka John Blake, relate a story about The Who. 'John Creedon read out a piece about Keith Moon playing at Newbury in England only to get hit by Pete Townshend's guitar. I wrote up a piece about it from my memory and John read it out live on air. I thought this was amazing – this was the rock 'n' roll of radio.'

However, it wasn't until seven years after the O'Regan brothers' venture that pirate radio got a permanent foothold in Cork. Other fledgling stations had come and gone, including Radio Sundown which was broadcast from Blarney Street. But it was with the advent of CCLR and Cork Broadcasting Company (CBC) in 1978 that pirate radio took its first fledgling steps towards becoming a serious rival to RTÉ for Cork listeners.

CBC was the brainchild of DJ Daniels (whose real name was Don Walsh and who broadcast as Dave Porter) and Stevie Bolger. Don was a DJ and ran a successful disco supply shop on MacCurtain Street. Stevie was a Dublin-born DJ who had moved to Cork to act as entertainment manager with a new club called Good Time Charlies on Caroline Street.

Together, they set up CBC with a shoestring budget and basic equipment, but a burning desire to have fun on air with the music they loved. Word spread like wildfire and both were astonished with the feedback they received from fans at their various club gigs around Cork. They were also inundated with applications and demo tapes from youngsters determined to carve out a career as a radio DJ. In one of the remarkable quirks of fate, some of the DJs who first became involved in CBC and its follow-up pirate stations in Cork would go on to rank amongst the biggest names in Irish broadcasting.

'I heard pirate radio was starting up in Dublin. I was based in Cork at the time and I thought, why can't we do this in Cork as well,' Stevie Bolger recalled. 'I wanted to play the music I liked and I knew a lot of people wanted to listen to the type of music that just wasn't being played on radio. They had to listen to Radio Luxembourg for what they liked.

'I got the idea and rounded up DJ Daniels who had a music shop on MacCurtain Street. He had the gear and that was a critical start. Con McParland could get his hands on transmitters which was another plus and, of course, I could sort out the "jocks". That is where CBC started. We had a bit of a falling-out a short time later – it was a bit like being in a band and the musicians rowing over the music not being good enough.'

CBC had an instant, astonishing impact on Cork's social scene. Its arrival on the airwaves electrified local youngsters who were desperate to listen to their favourite pop and rock music. If RTÉ was perceived as 'stuffy' and conservative, CBC was exciting, brash and willing to try new ideas.

Sometimes those new ideas weren't the best advised. On 17 March 1978, CBC used sports cars to participate in the St Patrick's Day parade to promote their station – and one CBC volunteer cheekily approached the parade viewing platform and proudly presented a record to then-Taoiseach Jack Lynch. The result was, just days later, the Gardaí and Posts and Telegraphs inspectors raided the station's studios and confiscated their gear. But the station defiantly found new equipment and stayed on the airwaves.

'Later, Alternative Broadcasting Cork (ABC) started up and it was really an alternative to Cork Local Radio which was only on for about an hour a day. We set up ABC in a flat at Farleigh Place in Montenotte. I found this house that was lying idle, contacted the guy who owned it and asked if I could it? From there, because Montenotte overlooked the entire city, if you ran up an antenna you could get a great signal across the entire city. Sure enough, that's exactly what we did,' Stevie added.

Don Walsh, aka DJ Daniels, admitted that no one could have predicted the impact that CBC would have on the Cork music and arts scene. 'CBC was basically Stevie Bolger, Con McParland and myself. We started in the small front bedroom of my mother's house at Wilton Gardens. Con McParland was the technical genius, and a very clever bloke he was. But, in my book, he was like a lot of other very clever people and ranked as a borderline lunatic. We did stuff together back then that Health and Safety Authority (HSA) officials would have a fit about today. For instance, putting aerials up by climbing along the roofs of five-storey buildings up in St Luke's without a harness – that kind of thing.

'I suppose a lot of what we were doing was groundbreaking. At that time your radio choice was RTÉ or RTÉ. As young whippersnappers we wanted to listen to the music we liked and that just wasn't being played by RTÉ. I was very much involved in the music scene, as was Stevie. We both knew what was happening in the UK with music radio and we thought what was happening in Ireland was balderdash.

'We said we would give it a try ourselves and that is what we did in Cork with CBC. I don't remember precisely how it ended up being the three of us but we set up the station and started broadcasting within a couple of weeks of deciding to do so. The draw for me was that I was a DJ and I wanted to try to do here in Ireland what DJs were doing across the water in the UK. You had stuff like Radio Caroline happening in the UK and it was all really exciting.'

Ultimately, CBC became a victim of its own success. The station simply wasn't set up to cope with the commercial challenges it would face through strong advertising revenues, staff costs, equipment investment and, eventually, its very success brought it to the attention of RTÉ, the Department of Posts and Telegraphs and the Gardaí. CBC also inspired other stations like Alternative Broadcasting Cork (ABC) to set up and their success, in turn, hit the original of the species.

DJ Rob Allen recalled the excitement with which CBC's arrival on the Cork airwaves was greeted: 'Back in 1978 I was thirteen and I remember reading an article in the paper about pirate radio station CBC starting up in Cork. I was in the North Mon and I was thrilled. I will always remember rushing home and turning on the radio, finding the right place on the dial and listening to pop music.

'I think Boney M was one of the groups being played that day. I was delighted because we had never heard anything like it before. It was my first memory of pirate radio and it wasn't long before I knew that radio was where I wanted to work. I listened to Radio Luxembourg and I suppose it is funny that so many "jocks" that emerged from that period had the common denominator of listening to Radio Luxembourg and copying the style of presentation of their DJs.

'I have to say that Radio Luxembourg got me into the industry – that is where I wanted to work. I submitted a tape at age thirteen to Stevie Bolger who was working with CBC. But I was too young, of course. So when I was sixteen I ended up doing stuff for CCLR back in 1980. It was being run by Shay Curran, who was known as Peter Martin on the air, and I happened to meet him on the steps of the studio at French Church Street. I told him I always wanted to be on radio; I knew I was young but I only wanted a chance. He told me to come in that afternoon and I was on air at 5.30 p.m.'

After CBC, the Cork radio waves registered a veritable tsunami of pirate radio station start-ups. There was ABC, CCLR, Radio Caroline, Leeside Radio, Radio City, WBEN, Centre Radio, NCLR, Sunshine Radio and Capitol Radio in the space of just six years. Two future start-ups – SouthCoast and ERI – evolved into what was locally termed 'super pirates' such were their funding, commercial impact and professionalism. Both would provide the blueprint for the licensed Cork local radio stations of the future.

CCLR founder Shay Curran, a native of Dublin, moved to Cork to open a record store with Pat Egan on Patrick Street called Rainbow Records. The move to pirate radio was a natural shift for him.

'I remember myself and Henry Condon climbing across a couple of roofs near Paul Street or Half Moon Street in the 1970s and trying to use a bit of wire as an antenna for a broadcast. Then a uniformed garda stuck his head through a skylight window and asked the two of us to come down off the roof. Someone had seen us on the roof and thought we were up to no good. I had to go down to the garda station to make a statement. But that was pirate radio in those days. The shop owner decided not to press charges because we were giving him a couple of months' worth of free advertising.

'In the early days a DJ wouldn't be hired because of the quality of his voice but the number of LPs he could bring with him to the studio. CCLR wasn't set up as a commercial enterprise, not initially at least. It may sound cool now but back then it was a bit of a gamble. Firstly, it was illegal. Secondly, there was no Internet so searching for the gear you needed was really hard. I was waiting for months for a guy to get me the gear I needed to start broadcasting and, in the meantime, CBC had come on air in 1978.'

'I eventually found a ham radio enthusiast, I gave him IR£100 and he built me a transmitter. Our antenna was stretched up over buildings on Patrick Street and, I think, on the roof of Roches Stores. I think we called it Radio Shandon because our signal was only going from Patrick Street to Shandon. But, over time, as the signal got better we put an advert in *The Cork Examiner* for what we called "an exciting new radio project". That was how we got started. There was a great buzz about it but, for me at least, a certain amount of paranoia because of the threat of Department of Posts and Telegraphs and garda raids. There was a certain amount of fear involved.'

CCLR eventually closed and Shay went back, in the mid 1980s, to his original job of graphic designer. 'Looking back I didn't get much out of it. I never pursued a full-time career in radio. But I only have to turn on a TV or radio station today to see our legacy because you have so many national broadcasters who worked or started out with CCLR. It was a training ground, a place to start for some really talented people. I'm very proud of that.'

But of all Cork's early pirate stations, perhaps Radio Caroline is remembered with most fondness. Radio Caroline was the brainchild of Mickey Daly from Togher. Mickey's life revolved around music and, inspired by the success of other Cork pirate radio stations, decided he would try his hand at his own station. It initially operated from a caravan parked beside his Togher home and his mother earned fame – and everlasting devotion from young DJs – for her kind insistence on bringing tea and biscuits out to the caravan during lengthy broadcasts.

Radio Caroline, like CBC, proved the starting point for some of Ireland's most successful broadcasters, including PJ

15

Coogan, Ken Tobin, Trevor Welch, Paul Byrne and others. All went on to greater things – albeit with Mickey Daly none too impressed with them leaving the station that gave them their first break. 'I was brought out and introduced to Mickey Daly and his mother,' PJ recalled. 'I said I want to be on the radio. He told me I needed a demo tape and a CV.

'I put a tape together, no problem. His mother gave me tea and buns while Mickey told me I was very inexperienced. But Cork were playing in a football match that Sunday and the phone rang at 7 p.m. on the Saturday night. My mother took the call and told me a fella called Michael Daly was looking for me. I took the phone and Mickey said he wanted to watch the Cork match and asked could I do the 4 p.m. to 6 p.m. slot? That was my break.

'After the show, as far as I was concerned, I was a total disaster. But Mickey seemed happy and I was asked back. I still remember the first record I played was by Freddie Mercury. Mickey later asked me could I do an hour in the mornings from 10 a.m. to 11 a.m. I looked at my college lecture schedule and thought I can do that. A couple of Sundays later, I was asked to start at 3 p.m. and I was told a very special DJ was starting work for Radio Caroline. Mickey Daly said it was Kid Jensen's younger brother, Scott. I then realised it was Trevor Welch from Togher who was no more a brother to the BBC DJ than I was to Freddie Mercury.

'Radio Caroline was a great place but the studio was hilarious. There were two turntables balanced either side of a table and a couple of milk crates balanced on bricks in the caravan with a hole cut in a wooden door for access. It was the most precarious thing I'd ever seen. The microphone basically had a foam lump stuck on it which was a kitchen cleaner with the scouring end cut off with a scissors. It was an ultra-modern American-style studio so we were told.'

Paul Byrne of TV3 recalled that Mickey Daly was one of the unheralded heroes of early Cork broadcasting. 'I don't think anyone realised it at the time, least of all Mickey, but he was giving Cork talent a break, a place to showcase itself. There were people who carved out careers in broadcasting for themselves that would never have been able to do so if RTÉ was the only avenue open to them.'

But if CBC, Radio Caroline and others demonstrated what could be achieved, others were slowly waking up to the concept of how much could be earned. SouthCoast began operations in 1982, shortly before ERI. SouthCoast was relaunched in 1985 and, from them until 1988/89, both it and ERI would dominate the Cork airwaves with a slick presentation style and a forensic focus on all matters to do with Cork. For the first time, Cork pirate radio stations secured business backers with, if not deep pockets, sufficient resources to invest in proper broadcasting technology and to develop the commercial opportunities that came their way.

John Creedon, now an RTÉ star, recalled the development of the 'super pirates' years after he had got his break with NCCR. 'A pirate station opened up called ERI. It was Eastside Radio Ireland and that's where ERI came from. It was in Ballycotton and was being run by Joe O'Connor. I gave him a shout and he said: "Yeah, come down and do a programme." So I did and I was the only Cork guy there. Before long, I was the gaffer.

'I was using Joe's car to go back and forth every day. I must say that I loved it – ERI developed into a much bigger station. It became very solid and moved into White's Cross, into Joe's place up there. It was quite a powerful station, good trans-mitters and you could even pick up the signal in Limerick, Tipperary and Kerry.

'It became quite a serious operation. It was turning over big money and people were being paid decent money. ERI became a big hit with the Cork public and within a year I became the programme director. I came up with some mad promotions that just seemed to work. I loved what I was doing but then that got nobbled because of planning problems over the mast and other things.'

ERI's great rival was the revamped SouthCoast. For many, SouthCoast managed in the mid 1980s to develop an atmosphere that has never since been equalled on the Cork airwaves. Its main star was Romano Macari who followed the unlikely route into radio from the restaurant business. His idea was that radio would be used to promote his food operation, Rocky's Restaurant. But his show on SouthCoast quickly developed a cult following.

'We had Pete O'Neill, aka Pete Andrews, and Rob Allen involved and, of course, Trevor Welch. We were broadcasting from upstairs. Rocky FM wasn't really the name to continue with. After a fire, we changed it into a fast food outlet and so we were talking about the radio station and, after considering it with Peter O'Neill, we said why not take over the SouthCoast mantle? That's how it came about. It would have been about the early or mid 1980s.

'Radio, we felt, wasn't really doing a service for the people of Cork. It was more than just playing the hits of the day. We wanted to give people a voice. People could come on, have a chat, talk about what was going on in their community and in the city. That's how the live phone-in was born with SouthCoast.

'People would talk about everything. We played requests for them and it proved a really popular format. We did it for a trial run and I decided to host that show because it was my brainchild. I don't think we ever believed it would be the phenomenal success it became.'

Fans still recall the magic that SouthCoast generated. Lilian O'Donoghue, née McCarthy, was a teenager in the 1970s who had a passion for music and for radio. Her favourite stations were SouthCoast, Radio City and CBC. She was so enamoured of the stations she compiled special tribute albums on each, ranging from photos of DJs to playlists and even memorabilia. Lilian visited the stations, noted memorable broadcasts and collected station logos and promotional material.

'I first got interested in radio when I met some of the DJs from CBC. That would have been the first week of August in 1978. I never looked back. I suppose no matter what station anybody goes into, they will always prefer their own local station. That goes for me too,' Lilian said.

Over the years, Lilian was welcomed into CBC, SouthCoast and Radio City as a fan and loyal listener. It was an era when disco was king and most DJs were lucky to be able to run old Fiat 127s or Ford Escort cars. 'My favourite station was SouthCoast. I loved listening to it. Of all the stations I've ever been to, I can say that SouthCoast looked the best. I suppose it helped that the station was only down the road from me. In the end, it became like my second home. I got to meet all the "jocks" and I had such great times listening to the station and getting to know the lads.'

Perhaps the importance of the pirate stations at that time is best underlined by a poem that Lilian included in her tribute albums to her favourite stations. 'Radio was my first love, it will be my last, SouthCoast of the future, CBC of the past, to live without my radio, would be impossible to do, in this world of trouble, my radio pulls me through.'

96FM sports editor, Barry O'Mahony, aka Mike Cagney, said simply calling in to a Cork pirate radio station in the 1970s and early 1980s could result in an impromptu broadcasting role.

'Neil Prendeville, aka Jim Lockhart, was involved with CBC and we were great buddies growing up. Music was our thing and, in particular, listening to Radio Luxembourg. We all dabbled in doing a bit of DJ work and that's where I fell in love with radio. Another friend of ours, John O'Hara, he was known as Johnny Gaynor of CCLR, was on the air and I knew a good few people in the industry. Neil asked me to come into CBC one day and I did.

'Pete O'Neill was working there and said to me that there was entertainment stuff to be read out on air and would I have a go at it? I said: 'Why not?' But he told me I needed a name. I picked Mike Cagney but little did I know that eventually within pirate radio in Cork you would have Mark Cagney and Mike Cagney. I read out the entertainment news and that was it – I was hooked.

'I can't quite recall how CBC finished up but I ended up with CCLR, where Shay Curran was the man. I had the radio bug by then and I decided that this was what I wanted to do. I consider CCLR to be where I *really* started and I've been working in radio ever since.'

Both ERI and SouthCoast posed, for arguably the first time ever, a serious challenge to RTÉ in Cork. Cork Local Radio, RTÉ's own Cork offering, had its fans but it never managed to generate the excitement of the pirates, particularly amongst younger audiences.

By 1988, both ERI and SouthCoast were highly professional outfits with paid staff, expanding advertising departments, the ability to operate outside broadcasts and both eyes firmly on the prize of an IRTC licence. The early laissez-faire attitude of pirate stations was long gone and both SouthCoast and ERI in the late 1980s were exceptionally professional outfits.

Both also faced a 'Catch 22' scenario – to have any chance of a successful license bid, they'd have to leave the airwaves as directed by the state agencies involved. But, at the same time, there was no guarantee of a license or that they'd ever be able to go back on the air.

CHAPTER TWO
The City

Looking back, 1978 was a turning point for Cork in so many ways. The optimism of the 1960s had rebounded after the setback of the oil-price-inspired recession of the early 1970s and better times seemed on the horizon again for both Cork and Ireland.

There was also deep pride in local sporting and cultural accomplishments. Cork's hurlers would achieve a famous three-in-a-row of All-Ireland triumphs in 1978. Cork's Gaelic footballers had lifted the All-Ireland football title in 1973 and boasted one of the county's best teams in decades. In football, Cork United was about to start up in the FAI League of Ireland to replace Cork Hibernians. Hibernians stunned Irish sport by having to quit the league in 1977 due to financial problems. This was despite the club winning the league in 1971 and the FAI Cup in both 1972 and 1973, the former thanks to a stunning hat-trick from Miah Dennehy, who was later sold to Nottingham Forest.

Cork's own Jack Lynch had been re-elected Taoiseach the previous year in a landslide general election victory. One of the first acts of the new Fianna Fáil government was to abolish rates, a move hugely popular with voters.

The profile of the city also began to change. Cork got its first US-style fast food restaurant in the shape of Burgerland on Patrick Street, soon to be followed by Pizzaland. The famous Woolworths outlet departed the scene but planning moves began to prepare for the city centre's first major shopping centre, Merchant's Quay, which would eventually open in 1988. Cork would also quickly secure modern suburban shopping centres in Wilton, Ballyvolane and Douglas.

City centre trade was still dominated in the late 1970s by names synonymous with Cork trade for generations – Roches Stores, Cashs, Dunnes Stores, Cudmores, Murphys, Fitzgeralds and Guineys. Ireland's oldest daily newspaper, *The Cork Examiner*, still proudly had 'Cork' in its title and was published and printed on Academy Street in the city centre where it had been based since the mid 19th century.

Thompson's Bakery was the dominant business on MacCurtain Street, from their famous red-brick headquarters. Their old electric delivery vans were still a daily sight, crawling up the incline of Bridge Street after a delivery route with just enough battery power to make it back to base. By 1984, even that sight would be consigned to history as Thompson's ceased operations on MacCurtain Street.

The period 1977–1980 also saw Cork react to increasingly heavy traffic congestion by launching a study that would, within a decade, transform the future growth and appearance of the city. The Land Use and Transport Study (LUTS) may have sounded incredibly boring but its impact on Cork is hard to overstate. Without LUTS, there wouldn't have been a South Ring Road, a North Ring Road and ultimately the €70m Jack Lynch River Lee tunnel and the development revolution it triggered for Mahon. Yet, in 1978 all those things were for the distant future.

Cork got its first pirate radio station that year in the form of CBC and, within a few months, ABC and CCLR. The pirates arrived, however, just as the economic and political mood began to shift, unfortunately not for the better. For decades, Cork's economy had been underpinned by several high-profile industrial and commercial heavyweights such as tyre manufacturer Dunlop, US car giant Ford, textile firms Sunbeam and Youghal Carpets, as well as Irish Steel and Verolme Dockyard in Cork harbour. In the late 1960s, those old-style heavy industries accounted for almost sixty per cent of direct industrial employment in Cork and almost seventy per cent of non-agricultural exports. There were few city-based families who didn't have some connection to the giant Cork employers.

However, by mid 1978, it was clear that all six were in trouble. Former *Irish Independent* southern correspondent, Sean Power, recalled the palpable sense of fear over the potential job losses involved. 'It was a time when a lot of the things people took for granted suddenly started to be challenged. People always assumed that firms like Dunlop and Ford would be around forever and that they would always employ hundreds if not thousands of workers.

'By the late 1970s, it was clear that this wasn't going to be the case. I think 1978/79 was the first time that, as the economic situation worsened, people began to realise that the entire local landscape was going to change. And that frightened a lot of people.'

First CBC and then ABC hit the Cork airwaves and they reflected the views, largely unvoiced until then, of a generation of young Irish people whose goals were very different to those of older generations. Many of them were also acutely aware that if the economic mood continued to deteriorate they would face a repeat of the 1950s, when emigration was the only alternative to years spent on the dole.

Ford was a case in point. It employed over 1,100 staff at its vast Marina plant in Cork and had, since the factory first opened in 1917 by Henry Ford himself (the descendent of a west Cork migrant), ranked as one of the most important employers not just in Cork but in Ireland. During the 1960s and 1970s, Ford cars had dominated sales figures like none other. As British car brands such as Triumph, Austin, Rover, Leyland and others struggled, Ford surged forward with bestselling models like the Anglia, Escort, Cortina, Granada, Capri and then Fiesta.

The exotic-sounding Capri was, for many young people, the emblem of an entire era. Pirate radio DJ Noel Welch, aka Noel Evans, put his life savings into purchasing an old Ford Capri. To this day, it remains the favourite amongst all the cars he has ever owned. 'It was the coolest car you could hope to own at the time in Cork. There were some who liked the Opel Manta but I think the Ford Capri became the symbol of that era. It was our answer to the Ford Mustang and the famous American sports cars that seemed to symbolise the 1960s.'

But, cool as it was, the Capri was nearing the end of its days in the late 1970s. Sadly, so too was the Ford plant which, for seven decades, had provided Cork youngsters with a profession. By 1978, Ford was about to phase out its bestselling Cortina model and introduce a radically new successor, the Sierra. Everyone knew that the future of the entire plant hinged on how successful the new car would be. The fact the new model was quickly nicknamed 'the jelly mould' because of its radically modern styling didn't bode well.

Job cuts also accompanied the new model as Ford sought to bring the costs of its Cork plant into line with other European car plants and cope with the challenge of Japanese cars, which were fast expanding their market share. 'Everyone hoped for the best for Ford in Cork but I think they feared the worst,' recalled Joe Walsh who was elected a Fianna Fáil TD in west Cork in 1977. The late Clonakilty-based TD would, over the course of his career, become Europe's longest serving Agriculture Minister.

Ford would struggle on for five more years before finally closing the Marina plant in July 1984. The workforce had reduced to 800, from 1,100 just two years previously. The impact on Cork was exacerbated by the closure of the nearby Dunlop plant in 1983 with the loss of 850 jobs. Put in context, from an employment perspective, in 1972 Dunlop had boasted 1,800 workers.

In a handwritten government memo dated 27 November 1981, an anonymous civil servant warned that Ford's Irish boss, Paddy Hayes, 'talks to G. (God) Almighty only'. The memo also set out a range of measures ranging from ministerial visits to the Ford headquarters in the US to IDA grant support aimed at keeping Ford manufacturing in Cork.

In a letter to the government on 23 January 1984, Mr Hayes stressed he was saddened by the closure announced on 17 January. 'I am sure that you [Dr Garret Fitzgerald] will understand that, apart from the 800 people losing their jobs, my personal regret and sadness is more intense that any other Irishman's could be.' Mr Hayes had written to Taoiseach Charles Haughey on 21 September 1982 warning that the future of the Cork plant and its workforce effectively hinged on the Detroit firm's successor to the venerable Cortina saloon which had been one of the best-selling cars in Europe for two decades.

'We attach great importance to the assembly of the new [Ford] Sierra because the future of Ford Ireland and its 1,100 employees depends to a great degree on its sales success both in Ireland and in Europe generally,' Mr Hayes wrote. He also invited Mr Haughey to visit the Cork plant.

Ford had invested IR£9m in the Cork plant, a major sum given what Mr Hayes warned was 'these troubled times'. The firm planned to export 16,000 Sierras a year with the new model, if successful, guaranteeing full employment at the plant. By 1982 Ford had told the Department of Trade its Cork plant was losing IR£10m a year due to the firm having to keep prices low to compete with Japanese imports, which were benefitting from the currency exchange between the yen and the dollar.

Ford was also planning major job losses at its Dagenham plant in the UK which was its major European production centre. In January 1984 Ford confirmed that the Cork plant would close with the loss of all jobs. Government hopes for some jobs to be salvaged through an auto components sub-plant came to nothing. Few doubted the impact on Cork and the entire economy of the south-west region.

On its own, the closure of the Ford plant was a major blow for Cork. But taken with the job losses in Dunlop, Verolme, Youghal Carpets and Sunbeam, it represented an economic catastrophe that has never since been witnessed. Irish Steel was similarly in deep economic trouble, but the Fine Gael–Labour coalition refused to allow it to fail given the grim plight already facing Cork industry. Instead, it was subjected to a slow, lingering death over the next decade.

Irish Steel/Irish Ispat eventually closed with the loss of over

400 jobs in 2001 and left Ireland facing the biggest toxic waste clean-up in state history. The closure marked the end of seventy years of Irish steel manufacture and also the conclusion to one of the most controversial state asset sell-offs. Founded in 1939, Irish Steel was – after years of losses – sold to Indian steel billionaire, Lakshmi Mittal, in 1996 for just IR£1. It marked an ignominious end to the state's ownership of the firm which began back in 1947.

Cork's energy sector had more mixed fortunes in the 1970s. The discovery of natural gas off Cork in the so-called Kinsale Head field proved a major economic stimulus, though predictions of it doing for Cork what North Sea oil did for Aberdeen proved wildly over-optimistic. It was offset by the tragedy of the 'Betelgeuse' disaster in Whiddy Island off Bantry on 8 January 1979. A total of fifty people died – forty-two French, seven Irish and one UK national – when the oil tanker exploded during an operation to unload its cargo. Oil operations at Whiddy were dramatically reduced in the following years, though the facility remained open.

It is hardly surprising that all these grim economic tidings impacted on both the mood and confidence of the city. In particular, it sparked a search for escapism amongst the local youth. The certainties their parents had enjoyed were slowly being challenged both in economic and social terms. Looming large and dark on the horizon for every teen in the late 1970s and 1980s was the threat of the dole queue. For thousands the only alternative was the ferry to the UK or a flight to the US, Australia or Europe.

Some in Cork turned for escape to sport, others turned to music. For many, pirate radio offered a route out of local troubles, at least for a while, and DJs knew precisely what

Corkonians were talking about. They were also stations dominated by local news and social developments and manned by DJs that revellers would meet in Cork clubs on a Friday, Saturday or Sunday night.

The major difference between Cork and Dublin was that, while both endured economic hardship at the time, it was from the capital that successful major Irish rock acts emerged, many inspired by the social hardship they had witnessed. The 1970s and early 1980s produced such globally successful Dublin groups as U2, The Boomtown Rats and Aslan as well as The Radiators, The Blades, The Vipers and The Virgin Prunes. They were later followed by Something Happens and The Frames. In Cork, the greatest success was enjoyed by Rory Gallagher and, later, by The Sultans of Ping and The Frank and Walters. The latter clearly never rivaled the success of the great Dublin groups. But trad-folk outfits Nomos and The Stargazers gave Cork one of the city's best-loved singer-songwriters in the shape of John Spillane.

Ironically, it was the closure of the Ford plant, and the desire by the US car giant to mitigate the public relations fallout from the decision, that led to one of Cork's most beloved music events, Siamsa Cois Laoi. The music festival, sponsored by Ford, ran for around six years and proved wildly popular, attracting acts such as John Denver, Kris Kristofferson, Joan Baez and The Pogues. Despite its departure in the late 1980s, it laid the groundwork for the Live at the Marquee summer concert series launched in 2005 by Peter Aiken, which has established itself as one of the world's most highly regarded musical events. Fittingly, it is located just metres from where Siamsa was staged in the 1980s.

SouthCoast's Romano Macari said part of the incredible

success of pirate radio in Cork in the 1980s can be directly traced to local economic concerns. 'Back in those times you had Ford, Dunlop and Verolme Dockyard. There were a lot of closures, job losses and a bit of a depression in Cork at that time. The unemployment rate in Cork at that time was really high. I think it was running about twenty per cent or so. There were loads of people out of work.

'I don't think there was a family in Cork that didn't have a relative or friend who hadn't lost a job. Those were the times people were living in. But I think in SouthCoast we tried to turn the negativity around the city into something positive. We offered a sympathetic ear. Remember, we weren't a station in Dublin pretending to know about Cork people and their problems – we were right in the middle of it.'

SouthCoast decided to mark the Cork 800 celebrations, designed to mark the anniversary of the city's founding, by setting a target of helping to get 800 jobs for people. 'Those were the kind of things that made pirate radio stations in Cork different to the established stations in Dublin. And I think Cork people appreciated the difference. They liked the idea of having their very own radio station.'

Paul Cassidy, a school friend of Henry Condon, said Cork's love affair with pirate radio was as much to do with the county's DNA as the social impact of the era. 'Cork isn't known as the Rebel County for nothing. There was something about pirate radio that attracted young people – the fact that it was illegal and that they were playing music that older people didn't want you to listen to. CBC was my first memory of pirate radio in Cork and I thought it was a very good radio station. I was sixteen or seventeen years back then and radio was magic. At one stage Henry and myself even ran a radio station from an attic in his house in Montenotte and we called it Radio Atlantis. It only broadcast to our own school but that's the level of interest there was in Cork in radio.'

96FM's Derry O'Callaghan said local teens like himself were initially astounded that such quality radio stations as CBC could be broadcasting from Cork. 'When you are really into music, when you love radio, to realise that this was happening in your own home town was actually beyond belief. I don't think you can overstate the importance pirate radio stations had for the people, particularly young people, in Cork back then.'

For Derry, who now hosts the wildly popular *Oldies and Irish* show on 96FM, radio assumed enormous importance in an era before Internet, music downloads, MTV and satellite TV. 'It is hard for young people today to understand because they have so many outlets for music. But for us pirate radio was a lifeline to the music we loved.'

Pete O'Neill, aka Pete Andrews, formerly of SouthCoast, said CBC was to Cork what Radio Caroline and Radio Luxembourg were for the UK. 'There were some really big names from the Cork scene there at the time. There was Mark Cagney, DJ Domino and John Craig. It was also my unfortunate pleasure to be live on air for the first raid by the Department of Posts and Telegraphs. I called DJ Daniels at his shop on MacCurtain Street and told him we were being raided. There were about twenty Gardaí and guys from the department banging on the door. I ran up a side door and, as I left the building, the door to the basement was being knocked in. It was a very close call.'

Yet it wasn't long before CBC, CCLR and others gave way to the 'super pirates' of the mid 1980s. Their growth mirrored the re-emergence of the city after almost a decade of economic gloom. Despite the death of old, traditional industries the seeds of Cork's future economic comeback had already been sown. Pfizer was expanding in Ringaskiddy and, by 2005, would ultimately grow to operate four major production plants in Cork. By 2000, Pfizer was manufacturing Sildenafil at Ringaskiddy, the key ingredient, or 'rising agent' as the wits described it, in the global drug sales phenomenon that was Viagra. By weight alone, Sildenafil was worth more than gold.

The success of Pfizer in Cork also attracted other pharmaceutical giants. By the early 2000s, Cork would rank second only to Switzerland as a concentration of major drug production. The firms operational in Cork would ultimately expand to include Novartis, Johnson & Johnson, Eli Lilly and Schering-Plough. Through direct and indirect employment, over 20,000 Cork jobs would be supported by the pharmaceutical-chemical sector.

The other major breakthrough Cork enjoyed was persuading California-based computer firm, Apple, that their European manufacturing hub should be located on Leeside. Apple first opted for Ireland and then opened their new plant at Hollyhill in 1981. Its employment soared to 1,500 as Apple, like Dell in Limerick, enjoyed incredible worldwide sales success. Apple then decided in 1998 to move its Printed Circuit Board (PCB) operations to Indonesia. By 1999/2000, Apple decided to move iMac production from Cork to the Czech Republic and Korea, resulting in over 450 redundancies. Many predicted it was the modern equivalent of the Ford and Dunlop wind-down.

But Apple proved the doubters wrong. The firm focused on sales support, research and development and administration rather than simple manufacturing. Within a few years of losing iMac production, the firm began to expand its workforce once again. That expansion was underpinned by a range of record-breaking new products ranging from the iPhone to the iPod and iPad.

Today, Apple employs over 4,500 staff, more than double its peak of the mid 1980s. It is also considered the most important base for Apple outside their Cupertino headquarters in California. In a development which reflects Cork's economic re-emergence, Apple's European headquarters is run from Hollyhill by a Cork woman, Cathy Kearney.

Cork Business Association director James O'Sullivan said it was interesting to note that the economic turmoil of the 1970s and 1980s had left Cork with an impressive local media structure and an employment base more diversified than any other Irish city, excluding Dublin. 'I don't think you can talk about Cork in that period without mentioning pirate radio. It was hugely important and its success was that it played to the sense of independence that Cork always had. CBC, CCLR, Radio Caroline, ERI and SouthCoast Radio weren't just pirate radio stations – they were Cork pirate radio stations.'

CHAPTER THREE

John Creedon, aka Eric Hansen, aka John Blake: 'My earliest memory of pirate radio was listening to a station based up around Blarney Street called Radio Sundown. I was only a young fella at the time, maybe ten or eleven. My older brother Don and my sisters, who were all really big into music, used to listen to it. It just seemed so magical.

'I subsequently discovered that one of the main movers behind it was Kevin Healy who went on to become a director of radio in RTÉ. He told me about this many years later. At one stage he told me that a guy announced that they had to go off the air because his mammy needed the kettle lead from the amp.

'I suppose from that I went on to listen to Radio Luxembourg and there was that fascination with a world of music, festivals, babes and long hair. For a couple of years in the mid 1970s, as a teenager, I used to hang around with Henry Condon in the city centre. Henry and myself were mad into music and the whole idea of pirate radio, even though there really wasn't much pirate radio in Cork at that stage.

'We'd go down to his house in Emmet Place and plug in a record and listen to B-sides and all kinds of exciting stuff. I suppose it was the sounds of the seventies – making tapes and listening back to them. Looking back now I realise that it was a great training ground once you got over that initial thing of listening to your own voice.

'The next thing the word went out that there was a pirate station starting up in Cork. Henry came to me and he was all excited about it. "It's only down the road from me – it's on Paul Street." We were probably no more than seventeen or eighteen at the time.

'We went down and met Shay Curran and convinced him to give us a go. Ber Horgan was Shay's partner at the time and they were involved in selling a bit of advertising. But that was how it started for me.

'You'd go up the steps on French Church Street. It's funny walking around that part of the city for me even today. I was involved with CCLR for a while but there was very little money in it.

'The next thing CBC opened. CBC was bigger, flasher and was basically the enemy. All we had were rehashed old jingles from Radio Caroline and stuff like that. They were very posh and brought down DJs from Dublin and London. We were going to be hammered – that was it.

'But I never moved. I was loyal to the very end with CCLR. The next thing there was a split in CBC when Don Walsh, aka DJ Daniels, and Stevie Bolger split. Stevie opened up ABC, which was Alternative Broadcasting Cork. It was a third player in the market and I didn't feel like I was abandoning ship. CCLR closed down shortly after and I went up to ABC and got a start up there. I was with them for a year or two and, in fairness to Stevie, he is a real romantic but also very genuine. I was getting, I think, about IR£5 a week. But I was so full of my own importance I used to get a taxi home to St Luke's from work, so I spent virtually all my money on cabs.

'I was a year or two there. I was there – on the air – when we were raided and there was really no coming back from that.

Stevie was going to fight it in the courts but there was always some sort of problem, a bum transmitter or some guy would be leaving. It got very complicated and the station just limped along until it fizzled out because of the raids.

'I got married and we had our first child. So, at twenty, I was out of the whole scene and it was kinda over anyway. I was down in Youghal Carpets but lost my job there. Then a pirate station opened up called ERI – Eastside Radio Ireland. It was in Ballycotton and was being run by Joe O'Connor. I gave him a shout and he said: "Yeah, come down and do a programme." So I did and I was the only Cork guy there. Before long, I was the gaffer.

'I was using Joe's car to go back and forth every day. I must say that I loved it – ERI developed into a much bigger station. It became very solid and moved into White's Cross, into Joe's place up there. It was quite a powerful station, good transmitters and you could even pick up the signal in Limerick, Tipperary and Kerry.

'It became quite a serious operation. It was turning over big money and people were being paid decent money. ERI became a big hit with the Cork public and, within a year, I became the programme director. I came up with some mad promotions that just seemed to work. I loved what I was doing and then that got nobbled because of planning problems over the mast and other things.

'I had to leave to get a job. I went to America because I didn't want to let go of radio. I was a cleaner in Penney's for a short bit but radio was where my heart was. In America, I tried to get into radio but I had no real luck. I went to Madison Avenue in New York in my threadbare old jacket and paraded myself up and down with thirty demo tapes, thirty CVs and thirty dollars in my pocket to try and get a gig. I did get one small job offer out of that from a station in New Jersey. But it was no job.

'I came back to Cork and, when I arrived, I got a phone call from 2FM asking would I audition for a show they were about to start with Val Joyce. They said needed a presenter in Cork and I was thrilled because I thought this could be my break. It was a bit of a back door for me because I was too late for one of the main gigs with 2FM which was just opening up.

'I was all set to audition when I got a phone call from the producer Pat Dunne two days beforehand to say: "I'm terribly sorry but we have to cancel." I said no problem we can arrange another date. But he said we couldn't go ahead with it at all. Some people in RTÉ Cork said that if I crossed the threshold they would put a picket on the door because I was a pirate. I said I was a former pirate but he said it made no difference. I explained that I'd left pirate radio a year ago so that I'd have a clean slate for anything that came up in RTÉ but he said it wasn't going to happen. He was in Waterford, I think interviewing Geoff Harris.

'I just felt it was very unfair. What had I done wrong? A load of the Dublin DJs, like Dave Fanning and Gerry Ryan, had backgrounds in pirate radio but in my case the problem was local in RTÉ Cork. Local staff had made a stand and warned that I wasn't to be allowed inside the door.

'I was left trying to make a living with my wife and small kids. I was working in factories, drawing the dole and trying to find some work. I ended up in Radio City in the 1980s and that was really important for me because I was able to stay in radio and pay the bills.

'It was great fun and a great place to be. But that closed down and I went back into factories. In 1986 RTÉ Radio 1 advertised. That 2FM experience back before my Radio City days didn't put me off and luckily things worked out for me.

'I often think that pirate radio was part of us growing up as a nation. You can drive conversation underground but you will never stop the Irish talking, that's my take on it. In terms of myself, pirate radio was absolutely brilliant because it kept me in touch when radio was untouchable.

'Back then, radio was essentially about middle-class Dubliners – it was made by them and it was run by them. No matter how brilliant you were, if you spoke with a west Kerry accent you weren't really going to get anywhere. For me, pirate radio kept me going. It was a bit like having a blank canvas and a box of crayons and being left at it for six years. You develop something.

'Cork was a hotbed for pirate radio and I think that was down to the fact there was always a free spirit about Cork. Even lads that came here from Canada, the UK and even Dublin recognised that. They found Cork very liberating – it was a very tolerant and welcoming city.

'Not only is eccentricity tolerated in Cork, it is actually celebrated. To be a character, to be a bit different, to be a bit of a madman, to be on pirate radio in Cork back in the day, it was taken as great. It might have been frowned on in other places.

'DJs got involved because they loved the music. Today, if you go into broadcasting you are basically streamed. You go to a journalist college, you hang out with journalists and you do journalistic things. But for pirate radio, people came from all kinds of different backgrounds and you learned everything from the height of masts to how to make and sell advertising. If it involved an outside broadcast, you were not only presenting the show but probably holding two bits of wire together in your hand trying to keep everything going. It was a root-and-branch training that you never forgot.

'There were some who saw radio as an opportunity to make money but, for the most part, it was all about the love of music and love of the job. You wouldn't have drifted into the industry if you weren't into that whole music scene in the first place. It definitely attracted people who were a bit bohemian. You took the risk of getting on the wrong side of the law and you also ran the risk of not being paid. Pirate radio was always on the edge.

'That was part of what the names or "handles" were all about. Because it was basically illegal, you never broadcast under your own name. I picked John Blake because it was my mother's surname. But we would make up names at the drop of a hat. I remember one day finishing my programme and being asked to read the news. I can't go on as John Blake so I read the news as Eric Hansen.

'All I wanted was to work in radio, ideally at the creative end. I never, ever thought: "My God, I could get loaded if I keep at this." That was never it. All I wanted was to be able to pay the bills and work at something that I loved doing. Working in local radio in my own city, for me at least, was the grooviest thing you could ever ask for. To end up on RTÉ Radio 1 for twenty-seven years was a bonus. I'm a bit Buddhist about it really. As you get older you look back and see, yeah, that's the boy in the man. That's how it worked out that way.

'I have twenty-five nieces and nephews and virtually all of them are in the arts. It was never a plan. It just happened. I think the gene inside me would never have been happy unless I was working in a circus or a theatre or a radio station. My mother never encouraged that but I was drawn towards it all.

'It was how life was. That was Cork in the 1970s. I was always drawn towards the flamboyant or something outside the conservative norm. It was a time when if you were a good-natured, well-intentioned but flamboyant person you could still find yourself in trouble. People could be jailed for just being gay. A garda could give you a clip across the ear if he thought you needed it.

'I think Ireland has grown up a bit and has come through its adolescence, if I can call it that. But music and pirate radio played a big part, in my opinion, in that growing up process. It was an Irish generation kicking back and saying: "Hang on, why does it have to be like this?" For some people it wasn't just music but it was sport, soccer in particular. For some youngsters it was about saying: "No, I don't want to play GAA I want to play soccer." Cork Hibs was a massive discovery for me at ten or eleven years of age. These guys had long hair and tans and English accents and silky shirts and loads of 'old dolls' hanging around them. We'd never seen the likes of it.

'If you think about the music back then it was starting to explode on two fronts. From the States you had disco but from England and, to an extent, from Ireland you had a lot of rage coming to the surface and that gave you punk, heavy metal, etc. All of it was new and, for me, it was part of a young generation fighting back for personal freedoms.

'The music was more than just the songs. It was music as part of a greater process. Rory Gallagher was absolutely breathtaking. Just going down to Cork City Hall and, in the same place where the city fathers would meet, you'd see a fella from Cork with long hair goose-stepping across the stage and burning the place up with his guitar. We'd go mental and the bouncers would be freaking out trying to get us to sit down.

'There was a revolution going on and music was part and parcel of it. There used to be some great gigs in the Arcadia as well. I remember one night seeing the B Specials. At other time you had U2, Bad Manners and Thin Lizzy.

'It was our 1960s I suppose. Ireland didn't really have the 1960s – America did and Britain did. But we didn't. There were a few hippies in Ireland but for the most part they were just laughed at.

'Radio was male-dominated at the time. I think I was aware of it because I had eight sisters and four daughters. When I was in ERI as programme director I was determined to try and get women on the air. Back then amongst the only two black guys in Cork were working on ERI for me. One was the "Man Ezeke" from Jamaica who I got a gig first as MC on some of our road shows and then with a regular slot called the *Sun Splash Show*. We became great mates. There was a guy called Lester working in Burgerland at the time. He had a lot of rap stuff because he was from London. Everyone knew him as Lester Rap-a-lot.

'I put him on at night and his show was really something very different. I was always looking for something outside the normal circuit rather than another fella from Cork with a box of records. I actually found it very difficult to find female DJs. They just weren't out there at the time.

'But I got three women into the newsroom – Colette Sheridan, Cathy Dillon and Lucy Potter-Cogan. All three went on to great things. Colette is a journalist with *The Irish Examiner*, Cathy worked for *The Irish Times*, *Hot Press* and the rest of it, while Lucy went on to work in RTÉ television.

'Some things I regret. I remember being at a local radio conference in Tralee with Dan Noonan before the pirate stations were finally closed. Ray Burke was the Minister for Communications at the time. Even though I was pretty young, I lobbied him and explained about the talent in pirate radio. He said: "Oh don't worry, all of you guys will get jobs." But I felt, to be perfectly honest, that the people who were adjudicating on who should get licenses, and some of those who were applying for licenses, were the direct opposite to the people who were in the pirate stations. A lot of them were party supporters, big businessmen and it was all about the profits on offer. It was all about what would make money – not if Cork needed a soul music radio station.'

'The flamboyance went out of it. I often think that when you formalise anything, the magic goes. I think hurling is a beautiful game but I don't really have any great *grá* for the GAA as an organisation or the guys who wear the blazers. I'm a huge fan of Jesus of Nazareth. He was the coolest man that ever walked. He was gentle, he was loving and he brought some amazing ideas to the world. I don't let some guy in a frock in Rome come between me and him.

'Equally, I don't need the board of some local radio station telling me what is right and what is wrong or what records should be played or what market should be only targeted. You can keep it. That's why I was very lucky to have been with the pirates when I was and to have gone to RTÉ Radio 1 when I did. If I'm honest, I think RTÉ Radio 1 is about the only station I know of that has the openness and the honesty that marked out the pirates.

To be allowed to do what I believe in is a luxury that I am very lucky to have always had. If it goes wrong or if it is not working, you eventually get shifted. But that freedom of expression is a wonderful thing. The flamboyance of the pirates, the half-baked mad ideas that they tried out, all of those went. The stuffing was kicked out of them when it all became commercialised and all about the profits. Not every single station because there was a huge blanket of conservatism came down over local radio after the licenses were doled out. There was also a huge element of repetition because if a format worked and made money, everyone copied it.

'I'm not trying to be cynical but I believe that the free spirit died when the licenses were given out in 1989. It is amazing now to look back on it all. I think the stations reflected just how much Cork people love to talk and how proud they are of their city and county. There's a strong streak of independence here.

'Cork definitely has critical mass. I think that's due to the fact that Cork city is so far from the borders of the county. You can do everything you like in Cork – go to college, work, get married and follow every sport you can imagine. It has its own airport. The place is so big that some people even opt to take their holidays down in west Cork. For the best part of 200 years the place has also had its own daily newspaper. Cork is a very self-reliant place and the growth of pirate radio reflected all of that.'

CHAPTER FOUR

Mark Cagney, aka Mark Anthony: 'My earliest memories from working in pirate radio where when I was a club jock. I was one of three guys who had full-time gigs. Phil McQueen, called "The Beast" or "Beastie", was another. Then there was a guy who would have been very well known, DJ Daniels (Don Walsh). Vincent Hanley had a gig as well. He had been playing in Good Time Charlies. Then he got the gig with RTÉ and I went into the club after him.

'There were two or three of us at the top of the tree, so to speak, in terms of the club DJ scene. Stevie Bolger ran Good Time Charlies and he had some connection to pirate radio in Dublin. Himself and DJ Daniels must have had some kind of conversation and they decided to get a Cork pirate radio station equivalent up and running.

'DJ Daniels had a business that hired out decks for mobile discos and stuff. He had a shop on MacCurtain Street. So the plan was to have their own pirate station and it was going to operate out of a room over DJ Daniels' shop, the block just down from what is now the Everyman Palace.

'Stevie asked me and I said "OK". It was all a bit secretive because, at the time – people may not exactly remember this – there was a lot of cloak-and-dagger about pirate radio. It was illegal and the Department of Posts and Telegraphs, as it was known as at the time, were very strongly against it.

'It was a breach of the licence and it was considered to be a bit subversive. This was in 1976/77. I was told to go on and play my records like a proper radio show. I'd grown up listening to Radio Luxembourg and the BBC. So I said "fine, but what about the music?" They said bring and play your own records. There was no such thing as a playlist or anything like that. It was a case of: "Off you go, do what you want to do." It was a bit of fun for a week or two.

'But then I said: "Hang on a second, this is work and I'm not being paid for it." At the time I was making a fortune from clubs and the rest. I started asking questions about how long it was going to last for? I was told: "Well, we'll see." I think DJ Daniels took the whole pirate thing a lot more seriously than we did. But I had nothing to lose from it. He had his business and a very hefty fine if the Gardaí ever raided the station.

'There was a bit of a thrill at the start but, by week three of it, my father rang me and asked was I working in pirate radio and annoying the P&T? I asked him why and he said he got a call from a guy called Paddy O'Connor who was the engineer in charge of Union Quay at the time in Cork. My father had done loads of broadcasting for RTÉ going back the years and Paddy had rang him. Someone had told Paddy that the Mark Anthony on CBC was Mark Cagney who was the son of his old friend Johnny Cagney.

'He asked me what the story was? Then he told me that Paddy O'Connor wanted to talk to me. I began to think: "Whoa – this might not be so funny after all. There could be serious trouble involved here." There were all kinds of stories doing the round about pirates being fined IR£500 which was a hell of a lot of money at the time. That wasn't the lot either because you could have all your gear seized too.

'Because of my father's connection I couldn't ignore the request so I went over to see Paddy O'Connor. He was a short, squat man but he had an air of authority about him. I went into his office, he peered over his glasses at me and said: "So, you want to be on radio?" I said I did and he immediately asked me why I didn't call in to see him? I admitted that I didn't know it was an option. He told me to put together a ten-minute programme on anything I wanted, preferably young and adventurous, draw up a name for the show and call back with it.

'This would have been about February and he told me to be back to him by the 11th of March. He said they would run a ten-minute audition for me and see how I got on. But he warned me that, in the meantime, I had to get off what he called "that other outfit". I agreed and went back to the lads a little shell-shocked. I had dreams of working on RTÉ, Radio Luxembourg or the BBC, but that's what they were – dreams. It was the DJ equivalent of scoring the winning goal in the FA Cup final at Wembley for the team you supported as a schoolboy. I talked to my dad about it. I talked to my aunt who had done a lot of radio broadcasting in the US and she gave me tips about the whole thing.

'I went back to DJ Daniels (Don Walsh) and explained to him what had happened. I told him I wanted to give it a shot and, to be honest, there wasn't any hassle because I wasn't getting paid for the work I was doing for CBC at the time. I went back to RTÉ on the 11th of March, did the audition, and they were back to me a couple of days later and said they were very impressed and wanted to start me about two weeks later.

'I went to work for *Cork About* with RTÉ Cork Local Radio which had an opt-out from the national network which was the only one at the time. I joined them in 1977 and within eighteen months I had filled in for Mike Murphy in Dublin on *Morning Call* and also filled-in for Rodney Rice. Shortly afterwards 2FM started and I was asked to join that.

'When people talk about pirate radio today they are mostly what we would call 'anoraks'. People are fascinated by that whole era and radio. They can tell you everything about radio, from what type of transmitters they used to who built the boat they transmitted from. I never had an ounce of interest in that stuff – I was only ever interested in the music and getting to play the music I liked.'

'I wasn't in the classic 'anorak' mould and I had no real interest in being a rebel and shouting at authority because I was a pirate. To be honest, I thought some of it was very silly coupled with the fact we weren't making money so how were you supposed to make a living at it? Mrs Cagney didn't raise a fool who would work for nothing, if you know what I mean? What I saw was career, money and future. When the opportunity presented itself in RTÉ I treated it for what it was – the chance of a professional career. I grabbed it with both hands.

'The only one of my generation who had gone through pirate radio was Vincent Hanley. He went up to Radio 1 and had become a bit of a radio star because he was doing big gigs like *Music on the Moon* and stuff like that. He was filling in for Mike Murphy, Gay Byrne and Brendan Balfe. Pat Butler was also working from the station (RTÉ Cork) but I don't think he had ever done anything in pirate radio.

'Michael McNamara was there and he was doing a few bits in Limerick and I think he got a few fill-ins. But myself, Vincent and Michael were the only ones from down here that made the jump. But when 2FM started up I think RTÉ plundered the two major Dublin stations and that is where Marty (Whelan), Ronan (Collins) and Dave Fanning and others came from.

'When 2FM started up it was mostly made up of those guys, with Vincent being the main anchor in the morning. Michael, myself and Geoff Harris from Waterford – we had the rest of the roster. I wouldn't have been very aware of them because I was involved in clubs and then in bands. Radio for me was just another way of playing music. I didn't really start out thinking about being a broadcaster. It wasn't until I went in to RTÉ and people like Paddy O'Connor and Máire Ní Mhurchú talked to me.'

'When I arrived at Union Quay there were three new producers who had started, Aidan Stanley being one. He became one of my best friends and we're still mates thirty-seven years later. They were the next wave in RTÉ.

'The only other person I know of that came through Cork was John Creedon and John didn't come through until the 1980s and he was about ten years younger than me. I don't even think he was involved in pirate radio when I joined RTÉ. There was no SouthCoast or ERI in Cork at that stage – they all came much, much later.

'I moved to Dublin in 1980 and commuted up and down for the first few years but then I got a TV gig when Network 2 started up. When I left Cork I basically had no connection with the local scene. If I'm honest, I had no real interest. I'd come back down and some friends who were kind of on the periphery would chat to me about it. But they were the generation behind me and I didn't know them personally. I was also very busy with what was going on for me in Dublin.

49

'I went to RTÉ in 1977 and was up and down quite a bit for the first few years. But I lost touch with the Cork radio scene. In fact, the first time I ever heard Neil Prendeville was in Dublin – I think he was with Capital/104FM at the time. I only got to really know these guys when they became legitimate; when commercial radio came in from 1989.

'What pirate radio did for me in the three or four weeks I was there was that it got me noticed by Paddy O'Connor in RTÉ. It was a door that opened for me. I didn't really learn anything from the pirates because I wasn't there long enough and pirate radio was literally two mobile disco turntables in a grotty room over DJ Daniels' shop. There was no playlist, no structure – it was literally a fella with a bunch of records who liked music, with a microphone and no idea if anyone was listening to what he was doing.

'There was no feedback because there were no phones. You just went on, as we say in Cork, acting the langer and finished the show. If pirate radio wasn't there, I'm sure that a lot of the guys that came later would still have made it through because of their talent and persistence. But as a shop window it certainly helped a lot of people. In my experience, the really, really good people will make it through no matter what.

'I left RTÉ and went to 98FM. They and 104FM were the two super local radio stations in Dublin. They were born out of the two super pirates in Dublin. It was a bit of an eye-opener for me because it was very formatted. I had a record collection of 20,000 albums and God knows how many singles. We were limited to a playlist of between 300 and 500 songs. The move was entirely for money. I did make a lot of money from the move and it kind of set me up but it was a very unrewarding experience from a personal point of view. It was very limiting and a lot of the heavy formatted music radio, well, a monkey could do it. That is no disrespect to the people that are in it. That is what the job required.

'Outside the breakfast slot, everybody is effectively running to format. I was lucky in that I got my show a bit off format. But Ireland is different. I've seen international programme directors from Australia, the UK and the States absolutely baffled by the Irish market. They couldn't understand how the biggest audience was mid-morning and Gay Byrne was the king. They kept saying: 'But this isn't the way it is supposed to be?' And we'd tell them that this was Ireland and this was how it was and they'd better deal with it.

'I caught a break with 98FM when RTÉ went on strike and a lot of people checked out alternatives to the shows they normally listened to. We managed to hold on to a lot of people that checked us out and why wouldn't we? We were giving away IR£1,000 every hour in competitions which had never been heard of before in Irish radio. That's a pretty big carrot for an audience.

'I should have left after three years but the money was so good I couldn't walk away from it. I stuck with it for another two years and then they said to me that I was obviously bored stupid with it but asked me whether I'd fancy stretching myself with a bit of talk radio? There was a really popular chat show at the time in Dublin with a guy called Chris Barry. They (98FM) said the only place in the programme where they don't win is against Chris Barry. They asked me whether I fancied taking him on? I said grand, they made me a nice offer and I gave it a go. But he was so well established that he kicked my ass up and down Grafton Street. He handed me my head on a plate in terms of competition. We just couldn't get anywhere near it. We did it for two years and said, "this isn't working."

'They said: "Look, you're not going to go back to music and

format stuff." They said we are going to have to let you go, so effectively Denis O'Brien fired me. But it was all very amicable and I have to say he really took very good care of me in the end. So much so that I didn't have to work for another year or a year and a half. Which was grand by me. I had done very well for the previous five, six or seven years and I was pretty comfortably off. During that year I did a lot of voice-overs and that business was going very well.

'Some of the people who had been involved in the start-up of 98FM had then moved on to Radio Ireland which was obviously in dire trouble. They decided on a format change from Radio Ireland to Today FM and the people involved, Dave Hamilton and others, were looking for somebody who had some understanding of commercial music radio. I got a call from Dave and he asked me for a chat. It was about a year after I left 98FM. I started and had a great two years with them.

'Then there was a lot of buzz about what was going on in TV3. Andrew Hanlon, who was the boss in TV3, had been the news editor in 98FM. We started out together and I was having a chat with him one day and asking about TV3. I was having a nose around, a bit of fishing, and he told me about this breakfast programme they were talking about and he asked me would I be interested? I said: "Why not?" I went down to do the audition, more out of curiosity, and, within two weeks he came back to me and said the gig was mine.

'That is more than thirteen years ago now and I've been with TV3 ever since. I don't really listen to a lot of music radio anymore because, to be honest, the format style bores the arse off me. I listen to Newstalk and Radio 1. They're my radio habits. I used to always listen to Gerry Ryan – I was a huge fan of his for twenty-six years but sadly he is no longer there anymore.

'I don't know whether it's a reflection of me getting older or what but, at fifty-seven, I am more interested in what is going on in the world now than what is going on with the charts.'

CHAPTER FIVE
The Music

The old joke goes that if you remember the 1960s, you weren't really there.

But no one could ever forget the 1970s and 1980s when it came to the sheer power and quality of the music produced. If the 1960s were about folk, pop, flower power and a redefining of a young rock 'n' roll, the 1970s and 1980s were decades of pure revolution. From glam rock to heavy metal, from punk rock to disco and from New Wave to hip-hop, the two decades were about a musical energy that had to be experienced to be believed.

MTV arrived with Vincent Hanley and suddenly pushed pop and rock to unparalleled commercial success. It was an era of socially conscious music, often angry, but delivered in such superb lyrical form that it transfixed the youngsters who heard it.

If the 1960s provided the music of the anti-Vietnam War movement, the 1970s and 1980s provided the soundtracks for the rebellion against the economic consequences of Thatcherism in the UK and the refusal of young generations to tolerate apartheid in South Africa.

Whatever musical rules hadn't been breached in the 1960s were well and truly smashed to pieces by 1979 – youngsters wanted to listen to their favourite music on Irish radio stations and not have to depend on Radio Luxembourg and Radio Caroline. Virtually every DJ interviewed for this book stressed that there was a direct link between demand for the remarkable music being produced in the 1970s and 1980s and the emergence of pirate radio.

Where the 1960s was the era of the showband, the 1970s was the time of the rock group. As the rockers dialled up the volume, youngsters abandoned the old dance halls and flocked to the live venues and discos that were now all the rage. The latter catered to those who wanted to dance to the new pop music that had evolved, in many cases from the Motown sound.

Disco reached its apogee in 1978/79 with *Saturday Night Fever* and the all-conquering BeeGees soundtrack. But disco had been slowly taking a stranglehold on Irish dance culture for years beforehand thanks to the work of Donna Summer, Michael Jackson and The Jackson Five, The O'Jays and even Abba. The Swedish supergroup dominated the charts from 1974–83 with songs such as 'Dancing Queen', 'Super Trooper' and 'Mamma Mia' amongst many more. They were augmented by a wave of 'Euro disco' bands such as Boney M.

Irish youngsters also saw nothing strange in dancing to Abba or Donna Summer in Chandras, Cocos or Zoes and then, the following night, heading to Sir Henry's or De Lacy House for a dose of hard rock or blues. The 1970s also saw rock 'n' roll evolve into even higher forms with the work of stars like Led Zeppelin, Bruce Springsteen, Pink Floyd, Tom Petty and Neil Young.

Ireland got in on the act with such bands as Thin Lizzy, Horslips, Rory Gallagher, The Radiators, The Boomtown Rats and ultimately U2. Cork teens flocked to hear the latest live acts at The Arcadia, City Hall, Sir Henry's and then De Lacy

The DJs of Cork City Local Radio (CCLR)

The DJs of Cork City Local Radio (CCLR) reunited in recent years

Neil Prendeville, aka DJ Jim Lockhart, in his younger days of pirate radio

Noel Welch's Ford Capri

Noel Welch, aka DJ Noel Evans, and his beloved Ford Capri

Noel and Trevor Welch having a laugh at the old radio set

Trevor Welch, Ken Tobin and Mick O'Brien, owner of SouthCoast Radio, on the North Main Street in 1985

DJs Fergal Barry, Rob Allen, Ken Tobin, Brian Gunn and Trevor Welch

Peter O'Neill, aka DJ Pete Andrews, in his pirate radio days

John Creedon, aka DJ John Blake, in the studios of Eastside Radio Ireland (ERI)

The flat at Farleigh Place, near St Lukes, where the studios of CBC were based in 1978

The premises which was the studio of Radio City in the early 1980s

The premises of SouthCoast Radio on North Main Street in the mid 1980s

Noel Welch on his first day on Cork Broadcasting Company (CBC)

PJ Cassidy at the mixing desk of Cork City Local Radio (CCLR)

A typical record library for one of Cork's pirate radio stations

Peter O'Neill with pirate radio enthusiast Lilian O'Donoghue, née McCarthy

Alan Edwards presenting one of his early pirate radio shows

Romano Macari with Noel Welch

Henry Condon and Ronan O'Rahilly, founder of British pirate radio
station Radio Caroline

House. But, above all, they wanted to be able to listen to their favourite music on their radios – something that RTÉ, at least until the roll-out of 2FM, pointedly was failing to do.

Steadily increasing consumer spending was also a crucial, if overlooked factor. In the 1940s and 1950s, a radio was a cherished and expensive item in family homes. People were lucky to have a single good set. By the early 1970s, cheap Japanese radios were flooding onto the market and it was nothing unusual for youngsters to have stereos in their bedrooms. New cars even had a radio. That was mirrored by the explosion in the number of record stores across Cork. Not surprisingly, pirate radio DJs were amongst the stores' best customers.

Cork pirate radio founder, Pete O'Neill, aka Pete Andrews, said it was seat-of-the-pants broadcasting which was powered by a sheer love of music. 'I got my surname "handle" of "Andrews" from a guy who told me I couldn't use my real name. He was sitting under a window in the studio, was obviously dying of a hangover and suddenly piped up "Andrews" because that's probably what he had just drunk to get himself right.

'I was on air with CBC when there was the first Department of Posts and Telegraphs raid. I grew up listening to Radio Luxembourg and the bad reception didn't spoil the experience of the music. I loved Larry Gogan on RTÉ Radio 1 – remember there was no 2FM back then – and he was my icon and hero because of his chart show.

'Looking back, the shows on pirate radio stations were really quite good. I think the fact the DJs were so into their music and took what they were doing so seriously shone through. And it was an incredible time for music. The 1970s and 1980s have to rank as one of the greatest eras for popular music. I did the *Favourite Five* show in the 1980s with SouthCoast. I remember at one point getting thousands of postcards from people, it was incredible and I remember being the envy of people on the station. I never looked for attention but I loved how radio worked. It was amazing. But it was really all about the music.'

Tony Magnier, aka Tony Vance, stressed that music was hugely important to youngsters and favourite bands were followed with an incredible passion. 'I used to tune into CBC and ABC and later Capitol Radio. I was also listening to Radio Luxembourg – I think almost everyone in Cork aged under eighteen was at that stage anyway. I absolutely loved the music. It was just great and you weren't hearing it anywhere else.

'It was so glamorous I decided I had to get involved, so I called down to Leeside Community Radio which was based down by Grand Parade over a flower shop. That was 1982 and you had all the great music from the 1970s and early 1980s on the turntable. I was seriously into music then and I was listening to Radio Luxembourg and BBC every night.

'My first record was "Pop Muzik" by M (1979) – I will always remember that. It was the first record I ever played on air. I wasn't paid a red cent at the time. I was actually putting money into my own DJ status because I was buying my own singles and albums to play on air. But it was all about the music for me. I thought I was the luckiest fella in Cork to have my own drive-time radio show and I could play the music I loved.'

Stevie Bolger, so instrumental in the pirate radio scene in Cork, stressed that the music of the era was a key factor in what happened. 'It helped that the 1970s and early 1980s was a great time for music. You only have to hear a song from that era on the radio today and you're transported right back. You had The

BeeGees, Status Quo, Michael Jackson, Thin Lizzy, Rory Gallagher, the whole punk rock thing and then the emergence of bands like U2.

'I remember the first time I saw The Boomtown Rats. They played a gig out in the Vienna Woods Hotel in Glanmire. There were only about twenty or thirty people there. But it was incredible. The first time I ever saw Rory Gallagher play was in Macroom at the Mountain Dew Festival. I just sat there, listened to the music and loved every single minute of it.

'A band for me was a lead guitarist, a rhythm section and a good drummer. I'm not really into this whole karaoke-backing-track thing that seems to dominate music today. Back then you were listening to really talented bands and you knew that some of them were going to go stratospheric because they had great material, fantastic stage presence and just gave off an air of excitement at their gig. There really is nothing like the buzz of a live gig.'

Jill St Clair, aka Pastricia Deeney, of CCLR was one of the very few women to work in pirate radio in Cork. She remains deeply proud of what she achieved – and how she proved that women were every bit as skilled behind a microphone as the male 'jocks' and equally adept at recognising quality music.

'I still have a letter at home from a girl who wrote to me in the 1980s. I absolutely loved it. She wrote to me: "Jill, you know, sometimes you can be quite good." It was a male-dominated industry at the time, some fellas did treat you with disdain and made it clear they felt you were "only a woman". There were times it was tough. I remember I played a disco one night and, when I played the first track, the entire place stopped dancing and everyone went silent. They just weren't used to female DJs.

'But I loved the music of the 1970s. I remember sitting up late at night in my bedroom with the radio turned down really low so my parents couldn't hear it. It was a very bold thing to do at the time, listening to pirate radio. I was kind of wild. You were a bit of a rebel if you listened to it.

'Funnily enough, my hero was Gay Byrne [RTÉ]. When I was sick at home in bed, it was his radio show that kept me company. It was such a great programme. Later on, I learned so much myself from working in radio.'

She admitted that the 1970s and 1980s were incredibly rich periods in terms of both the quality and variety of music being released. 'One song that I got right the first time I heard it – I said it was going to be a No. 1 – was "Video Killed The Radio Star" by The Buggles. That was in 1979. I think their video was the first ever shown on MTV. But they vanished after that one smash hit.

'I particularly loved disco music – it was such a wonderful period for great dance songs. There was Gloria Gaynor's "I Will Survive", The BeeGees with "Stayin' Alive" and "Saturday Night Fever", Donna Summer's "I Feel Love" and The O'Jays "I Love Music". And then you had Abba, who seemed to produce an endless succession of great songs such as "Dancing Queen" and "Mamma Mia". I think the quality of those songs is borne out by the fact that, if you go to a wedding or a party, people are still dancing to them today, thirty years later.'

Fergal Barry of SouthCoast echoed that opinion of the strange link between an incredible period of music and the surging popularity of pirate radio stations.

'You'd have a situation where a person might hear a song being played in a Cork disco and would then ring up the radio station asking for it to be played. But then the station might not have the single to play. There were record libraries in the stations by that stage but DJs would buy records, particularly the new singles, so the track might be in their personal collection and not in the station library. So you had to wait for either that DJ to play the song on their show or borrow it and play it on someone else's show.

'I remember that PJ Coogan used to bring in his own collection, quite an enviable collection, of continental hits. PJ was big into European music and things like the Eurovision. Rob Allen also had a great collection of 1960s music. I was a big U2 fan so I had almost every single thing they had ever recorded. Trevor Welch was also a huge U2 fan so you'd always get a U2 song on our shows.'

PJ Coogan, still an avid fan of Eurovision and the remarkable acts it produces, admitted that his favourite music remains the incredible material produced by Freddie Mercury and Queen in the 1970s and 1980s, ranging from the mega-hit 'Bohemian Rhapsody' in 1975 right up to 'Radio Ga-Ga' in 1984.

'It was just magical. I have never seen a live act like them. I was very fortunate to see them in Ireland and in London. They were simply breathtaking. That kind of music just inspires you and I suppose it is easy to see why youngsters were so determined to listen to bands like Queen on the radio. I still get a thrill hearing their stuff on the radio today, over thirty years on.'

Bob Stokes and Brian Gunn admitted that the love of music and the glamour of pirate radio were a hard cocktail to resist.

'I came to Cork in 1981 and I moved into a flat with Jerry Wilson and he was working in ERI out in White's Cross. When I was in Dublin I used to run discos with a guy at the

61

Castle Inn. I loved the buzz of the radio station. Then I heard through Jerry that the graveyard shift, from 10 p.m. until the early hours, was up for grabs in SouthCoast so I went for it,' Bob Stokes recalled.

'SouthCoast (the first incarnation) was about to collapse and I was only there for six months or so. But when it finally went I had got the bug and I was willing to go anywhere to work in radio.'

For Brian Gunn, it was similarly all about the music. 'I remember listening to ABC which was up in Military Hill and my bedroom used to look across to where their studios were. The music was fantastic and the DJs were really into what they were playing. Some of those programmes were absolutely brilliant because you knew that the jocks really loved the stuff they were playing.

'One day Paul Byrne (now TV3's southern correspondent) called me and said there was a new SouthCoast opening up on North Main Street. I couldn't wait to get down there and put in a demo tape. I will always remember Paul's advice which was: "Don't tell them you have never worked in radio before." That was the kind of era it was.

'The motivation for us was that we were listening to our favourite music from Radio Luxembourg or the BBC on crackly radio sets. SouthCoast then came on in crystal clear FM band and played all our favourite bands – it was like magic. It was pure class. The music was incredible. At that time, if you loved music, pirate radio was like a godsend.'

Neil Prendeville, aka Jim Lockhart, recalls how you could see the crucial linkages between the various trends, with youngsters wanting to listen to their favourite music on a local station and pirate radio then filling the niche. Discos provided

DJs with the income which pirate radio stations couldn't at that time and, in turn, the discos then fed off the soaring popularity of the pirate radio jocks. All the while Cork record shops were benefitting from a surging love affair with music amongst a younger population.

'Music was my thing. That's what drew me in to pirate radio. I had an insatiable appetite for music. I was hooked on pop and listened to Radio Luxembourg, the BBC and the *Top 40 Show*. The famous Tom Brown was on and I listened to his show religiously.

'My first record was Candi Staton's "Nights on Broadway". It was a 1977 hit so it crossed over into 1978 here in Ireland. I had been collecting records all the time. I don't think I was doing gigs at that stage. I was spending every penny I had on records from Ursula's on Oliver Plunkett Street, UNEEDA or Pat Egan's. I'm not even sure there was a Golden Discs in Cork at that stage.

'The 1980s were a brilliant time to be involved in radio and music. In many ways it was a golden era. I reckon it was arguably the best musical decade. It was so much fun. I think the 1990s fell off the cliff. Now, it is whatever you are having yourself. But the 1980s was a great time to be involved in radio because of the music.'

Brendan McCarthy, aka Paul Evans, pointed out that, to many youngsters pirate radio stations represented their entire access route to music. 'It is a different world today – youngsters have CDs, iPods, music TV, multiple radio stations and even music on their mobile phones. Back then, some kids had a radio, maybe a cheap cassette recorder and that was it. If you couldn't listen to your favourite bands or songs on pirate radio, you just didn't listen to them. If you wanted to tape a song, so you could listen to it over and over again, you had to wait for it to come on the radio.

'That is how important pirate radio was. It was a huge, huge thing in Cork. For many youngsters it was their first port of call for their favourite music. Not everyone had the money to buy singles or albums on a regular basis. So it was all down to pirate radio.'

Pat and Matthew McAuliffe, aka Ian Moore and Chris Edwards, said the demand for music quickly saw pirate radio stations trying to offer twenty-four hour music. DJs were also astounded by the manner in which they got interview access to some of the top acts which visited Cork.

'I remember in 1978, I was doing a few gigs at the time with a fella in school, Jim Collins, who lived up the road and he was starting up a new station called Capitol Radio. It was evolving from ABC. That's how I got started. I went on the lang from school and did my first show from the studio down on Tuckey Street.

'I will always remember that I interviewed Ian Dury of The Blockheads fame. It was 1979 and he came to play in the City Hall. I met him and he asked me was this my full-time job? I said no that I was helping out with a charity that worked with disabled children. He said "great, good for you". About half an hour later, there was a knock on the door of the studio. It was Ian's roadie with a big box of T-shirts to bring down to the lads where I worked, the lads with disabilities. For months afterwards all the lads were going around in Ian Dury and The Blockheads T-shirts.'

Michael O'Sullivan, aka Mike Kenny, said the arrival of pirate radio in Cork represented a musical landmark for the city. 'I remember ABC from the late 1970s – I'm not great on exact dates – but it was fantastic for the pop music it played. If you wanted to hear the hits of the day, you'd hear them played there. And there was nothing else. You might get BBC Radio 1 with a pop music programme but it was hard to pick up on a transistor. The pirates were providing a musical service and they were sowing the seed.

'My brother Fergus followed me into pirate radio when I was on CCLR. Like me, he had a huge interest in music – I think that was the starting point for all of us. We loved music and were really into the stuff we were playing on air. The start for me was when I was fourteen and I started listening to Radio Luxembourg with my brother, Finbarr. It was a big old valve radio and I will never forget listening to the stuff being produced in the early 1970s by Elton John, Rod Stewart and Queen. I developed a great love of music which, thank God, has never left me.

'I also loved the whole glam rock scene – great bands like Slade and T-Rex. For so many of us, it was a natural progression into being a DJ and working in pirate radio. For all of us, it was a total love of music. My start was in the Lamplight Bar on Barrack Street where I worked as a DJ with virtually all my gear in a suitcase.'

The musical theme is echoed by Philip Johnston, aka Philip Knight, of CCLR. 'I was really into music. I played in a band and spent almost every penny I had on singles and albums. I was working as a runner in Denis Walsh's clothes shop on Washington Street when I was a young fella. One day the girl from the advertising section of CCLR came in and I asked her how I could get into a station? She said to send in a demo tape and that's what I did – Peter Martin was station manager and I got a slot from 11.30 p.m. on a Thursday night.

'I actually picked my handle or pirate radio name from an Earth, Wind & Fire album. I was fourteen at the time. Music was my life – I didn't really play sport and I hadn't much interest in school. My band played in the Benson & Hedges talent competition in City Hall and pirate radio was the place to be at that time.

'I always remember the song that was playing in the background on my first day in the station – it was American soul band, Kool & The Gang, and their hit "Too Hot". There was some great music at the time. Derry O'Callaghan used to do the chart show – I remember him being there that day and we are still friends to this day.

'My first record was Blondie and "Call Me". I liked songs that had a good beat – maybe it was from my drumming background with the band. There was so much good music around. Every single week there seemed to be another great track being released. It's one of the reasons why it was such a great time to be involved in pirate radio.'

Pearse McCarthy, now of 96FM, said it is easy to understand why people are still so passionate about the music of the 1970s and 1980s. 'They were two absolutely amazing, incredible decades for music. There was no MTV but pop and rock music was still our life. It is hard to describe how important it was to have stations in Cork that were playing our favourite bands. For people who were teens in the 1970s or 1980s, I think pirate radio will always hold a special place in their hearts because it opened up the airwaves to the music people loved.'

Michael Corcoran, aka Mike Reid, of Capitol Radio and now of RTÉ said the combination of great music and mighty craic had to be experienced to be believed. 'The music was fantastic. The proof is that today, if I am driving and the window is open and a song comes on from the 1970s and 1980s, I will instantly know the musician. I can even tell you the album the single is from. People look at me as if it is strange. But it was such a great era for music. Some of the artists like Madness, The Specials, even The Bay City Rollers ... I adored the music of the era and I love it still.'

'It was a hobby for a long, long time for me. If someone had said to me back then that I could work full-time at it, I'd have said they were off their game. But remember we were all doing it as a hobby back then. RTÉ was the only legal radio station. So the only doors open for you were with the pirates. There was no formal training.

'Today, I go to third level colleges to talk to the students. The first question they ask me is where did I train? My smart-ass answer is that I went to the University of Life. I never had any formal training. We made it up as we went along. We made mistakes and learned from those mistakes. But we had the music and that is what mattered to us. Radio is a hugely powerful medium – probably the strongest in terms of communication. It is so instantaneous. Combine that with great music and you have some powerful communications tool.'

John Green, aka John Joseph, now with C103FM, was working as a bus conductor in the late 1970s but was fascinated by radio. 'I used to listen to Capitol Radio and was always interested in radio. Around 1979 they put out an advert looking for a presenter. I applied for it and got it and was working on the afternoon show from 3 p.m. to 5 p.m. The music at the time was really powerful and, I suppose, looking back on it so many people were really into music. They wanted to listen to their favourite songs and that is what pirate radio was playing for them.'

Steven Grainger, aka Stevie G, of Soul Jamz Records and Red FM, pointed out that, for many youngsters who couldn't afford to buy singles, pirate radio offered a chance to tape their favourite music. 'I remember listening to the radio in my bedroom in Grange with the tape recorder and trying to tape the songs and get rid of the DJ's voice. It is ironic, I suppose, because youngsters are probably trying to do exactly the same thing with me and my voice today.

'Romano (Macari) and SouthCoast was probably my earliest memory. It helped really get me into music, particularly the music of the day. There was everything from Springsteen to Michael Jackson and from Prince and Madonna to U2. Later on, ERI and the new SouthCoast arrived. It was exotic for us. If you were into music in any way there was no competition – you listened to pirate radio. MTV USA arrived in the mid 1980s but, until then, pirate radio was your only access to anything musically. It was pop heaven for us. It was a big thing just being able to listen to new music.

'I was buying my own records at ten or eleven years of age. I remember having a Manchester United jersey with the "Sharp" logo on it. A kid in school really wanted it and, looking back, the turning point for me was swapping it to him so I could get some money to buy the first three U2 albums. I had *The Unforgettable Fire* and *Under A Blood Red Sky* was out but I went and bought the earlier albums, *Boy*, *War* and *October*. The writing was on the wall for me when music took over like that. Pirate radio was a big part of that.'

Michael Lynam, aka Mike Williams, of SouthCoast said it wasn't just an incredibly rich period for the quality of music being produced but was rather noted for the fact youngsters appreciated the music all the more because it was so hard to access until the pirate stations came along.

'I remember CBC from when it started up. It was unreal at the time because the guards and the P&T lads would go to raid a station and not be sure about where the studios even were. I loved it from the very beginning. I loved the music and the sense that it was all local – all the stuff being broadcast was about Cork.

'I loved the music so much that, as a young fella, I used to go out cycling and I'd still have my radio dangling from the bike's handlebars. The music being played was like nothing we'd ever heard before on an Irish station. I eventually got my start with Radio Caroline thanks to the great Mick Daly. There was no such thing as training or playlists. I was told: "There's the turntable – just flake away." The music you played was entirely up to yourself. All I wanted as a youngster was to listen to music and play the stuff I loved on radio. It was an interest, it was a hobby – it was our life. The DJ who came on the Radio Caroline microphone after me was Jerry Newman, aka Alan Jones, and my God but was he good. He was even more into music than I was.'

CHAPTER SIX

Neil Prendeville, aka Jim Lockhart: 'My earliest memory of pirate radio in Cork is from about 1977 with CBC and Don Walsh, aka DJ Daniels. He had a small station on Patrick's Hill and it operated on AM, which is medium wave, 230. I think Mark Cagney was on the air with him as was Stevie Bolger. Vincent Hanley was also around the Cork club scene at the time. DJ Daniels himself was on the air and my abiding memory of the station was how weak the (broadcasting) signal was. It didn't have a great range.

'Radio Luxembourg was the main pop station, but there wasn't anything in Cork at the time which is what made CBC so exciting. It was basically the start of things to come. The first pirate station that I was involved in came on the air at the start of 1978. I got involved in February of that year, when I was seventeen. Music was my thing, that's what drew me in. I had an insatiable appetite for music. I was hooked on pop and listened to Radio Luxembourg, the BBC and the *Top 40 Show*. The famous Tom Brown was on BBC Radio 2 on Sunday nights at 6 p.m. on long wave with its dodgy signal and I listened to his show religiously.

'I remember making a homemade demo on an old tape recorder and sending it off to Shay Curran at a station called CCLR (Cork City Radio). At the time and they had studios up by the Mercy Hospital. They were in a tiny downstairs garret by a sweet shop called McSweeney's. The shop is only closed a few years now. On a Tuesday night in the middle of February Shay Curran rang my home and my mother put me on the phone. That was it – he said he had got my demo tape and he wanted me to come in and see him.

'It was amazing because that is where it all started for me. I was very nervous going in because while I had some records I hadn't an idea what I was supposed to do. You daren't tell anyone what you were doing because it was illegal and seriously frowned upon back then. But it was an amazing adventure and the start of really great times for me.

'The first record that I played on the air was Candi Staton's 'Nights on Broadway'. It was a 1977 hit that crossed over into 1978 here in Ireland. I had been collecting records all the time and was spending every penny I had on music from Ursula's on Oliver Plunkett Street, UNEEDA or Pat Egan's. I'm not even sure there was a Golden Discs in Cork at that stage.

'There was no such thing as a playlist. You had a fair old idea what to play because the station was into current pop. I was probably only on air for about thirty minutes at first, at 7 p.m. in the evening and I don't think too many people heard the show because the range wasn't great. You were a very long way from the 'super pirates' at that stage. It was very, very basic. There were two decks and a tiny mixer. There was a medium-wave transmitter in the corner of the studio that not only pumped out a signal but also radiation. It's a wonder it didn't kill us all.

'We were outlaws of sorts so you couldn't use your own name – that's why I picked Jim Lockhart as my "handle". I took it from the Horslips. The Department of Posts and Telegraphs, as it was back then, were constantly raiding us and seizing parts of transmitters, decks and even record collections.

It was all very cloak-and-dagger, we lived in fear of being arrested – hence the pirate radio moniker.

'In 1977/78, at the very beginning of the industry in Cork, we had to keep moving locations. You could say we were the original fugitives, one step ahead of the law. It was amazing because none of us were really paid anything. We went on radio out of sheer love for the music. I was like a lot of the others involved, in that I probably would have paid for them to allow me on air just to play the music I loved.

'The names were a bit hilarious because they came from all kinds of places: people's favourite football teams, snooker players, TV shows and even from comics. But you had to stay one step ahead of the officials.

CCR moved from Sheares Street to French Church Street and was rebranded as CCLR. Later Radio City opened on Parnell Place and all the while you had CBC operating on Patrick's Place.

'While we weren't getting paid at this time we all took it seriously. I practiced a lot. I would tape my show and then listen back to it on a small tape recorder at home. Radio was something I was very passionate about and was desperate to succeed at. To be honest, a lot of people that I worked with would have made really good jocks if they had decided to progress with it as a career, but they were working in different jobs and radio, for them, was either a hobby or something they did on the side. Some were butchers, some were driving for a living, some were salesmen, others were in college. It was a hobby for me at the start but very quickly I knew it was something I wanted to make a career of.

'I was studying accountancy at the time, which I absolutely hated. I suspect accountancy hated me as much. I did my first year or two on radio while I was still in school in the North

Mon. Some days I wouldn't go to school if I was on radio, I'd go on the hop. Or I might present a morning show on CBC from Penrose Quay from 6 a.m. to 8 a.m. and then go to school. Amazingly for the time, the radio station used to pick me up by taxi at home at 5.30 a.m. That didn't impress my teachers or my parents. I remember once after the school rang home to check up where I was, my mother called the radio station to check if I was there and I answered the phone to her!

'At seventeen I started gigging at clubs like The Carousel which was a weird kind of place to be for a jock who was so young, but they thought I was a lot older. There was a jock called "The Beast" and he was one of the stars at The Carousel and he got me a gig there. This was a long time before clubs like Cocos or Chandras opened in Cork. It was an 11 p.m. to 4 a.m. gig – but it paid big money, around IR£30. Some people weren't earning that in a week. It was great – all your music was supplied and all you had to do was turn up. This led to more gigs and pretty soon, with the combination of the radio work, I realised I could be onto a career path.

'The pirates were a great training ground for talent. CBC, CCLR, ABC, Radio Caroline, SouthCoast and ERI helped produce some really great jocks, a lot of whom went on to great success. By the time the super pirates emerged radio was very structured and already getting a bit formatted. You had decent newsrooms and the jocks were getting paid for the work they did. SouthCoast and ERI were even paying tax, so the Revenue Commissioners were getting their cut which was kind of weird given that they were still pirate stations.

'These stations gave people like me a chance to make mistakes and learn from them, we learned on the job. There were no opportunities at RTÉ at the time and they looked upon us in pirate radio with contempt. They never saw us as colleagues in broadcasting but more like second-class citizens to be looked down upon. RTÉ was effectively a closed shop. There wasn't 2FM until 1979 so all you had until then was Radio Luxembourg or your local pirate radio station. You had no opportunity to work and even when 2FM started all the jobs were hoovered up by Dublin jocks from stations like ARD, Radio Dublin, Nova and then Radio Sunshine. Dublin *was* Ireland and to some extent it still is. The funny thing was that there was money to be made if you had a regular pirate radio slot and were also willing to go gigging at night.

'The 1980s were a brilliant time to be involved in radio and music; in many ways it was a golden era and arguably the best musical decade. It was also a lot of fun. It gave me a fantastic life. Throughout my career I have made a good living in radio and consider myself blessed after almost four decades to be paid for doing something that I love as passionately today as I did when I started off in 1978. I have made some great friends and have had opportunities to make changes to people's lives in this city that I love through the power of radio. For that I will be eternally grateful.

'I did spend time on the dole in the early 1980s. There were huge queues and you had to sign on twice a week at White Street – awful stuff. It was a pretty horrible thing and I was very lucky to avoid all of that thanks to radio and gigging. Remember I didn't have a college education, had dropped out of my accountancy training and had a basic Leaving Cert. I was qualified for nothing so I was unbelievably lucky and I have been to this day, in spite of my mess ups and my mistakes. I've been extremely fortunate to have a career that I've loved and that allowed me to put bread on my table and a roof over my head. That's what pirate radio did for me – it gave me a chance to learn my skills, hone my craft and evolve from music radio into speech.

'ERI was the first of the pirates in Cork to delve into talk radio; up until then the pirates had concentrated on music. I was given the opportunity to present that programme and found that I really enjoyed it and had a bit of a flair for it. I even got to cover Wimbledon twice for pirate radio stations in Cork which was brilliant, once for ERI and once for SouthCoast. The grounding I got from speech in the pirates in Cork eventually helped me to get work in Canada. It was a very tough market to cut it in but I did it and when I had moved to Canada, I got another opportunity to go back to Wimbledon for CBC.

'I went to Canada because ERI was getting very messy. You couldn't get paid all the time. There were issues with advertisers and people from public life, from politicians to musicians and everyone in between who were being told by the mainstream media that if they advertised with us or gave interviews to us they would be barred by them. *The Cork Examiner* ran an anti-pirate campaign for years and of course their radio critics completely ignored the evolution of radio in Cork – they certainly were out of touch with radio listeners on their own patch back then.

'It was impossible to get press cards because we weren't welcome in the club, but despite being blocked for years by *The Cork Examiner* and RTÉ Cork local radio I eventually did get a press card through the NUJ in London. I could see the end coming and I felt I was going nowhere – it had become a bit like "Groundhog Day" – it was the same thing over and over but you were going nowhere. I was twenty-six at the time and I thought

I needed to do something to broaden my horizons. Everyone was leaving Ireland at the time because of the economy so it was no big deal. I was single and with no dependants.

'The US wasn't allowing anyone in to work on radio, they only wanted people for construction and the like. Australia was an awful long distance away and some dork in the Canadian Embassy told me they were hiring for radio personnel, which it turned out they certainly were not. I went to Toronto and soon found out it wasn't as straightforward as I thought. But I was lucky to meet some people in Cork who were living in Canada and gave me a place to live until I sorted myself out. I started working in Irish bars and hanging out in Irish clubs.'

'I used to hang out in a place called Mr Paykays where all the hot pop jocks drank. It was a very trendy kind of place, a bit like The Pitz or The Gay Future bar in Cork at the time. I got to know a lot of the guys, really talented jocks, and eventually they helped me get a job. But it was eight or ten hours away by train in northern Ontario. I did morning anchor news from 5 a.m. to 10 a.m. I worked my way there. The winters were very cold and very long and the summers were really hot. But I worked my way up to bigger markets and eventually back to the main market in Toronto again. It didn't pay as much as here because the industry was seventy/eighty years old and it was far more regulated.

'I did get to do a little TV over there and had a really good time. I think I always had a *grá* to come home. I would come back at Christmas and in the summer for a week or two. I loved Ireland and wanted to come back. As soon as they legalised the radio stations, I did come back. I was offered a job with Capitol Radio in Dublin which went on to become FM104. I was there for the launch.

'TV was never a particular love of mine. It is a nice medium but it is so slow and tedious compared to radio. It takes hours to set up and then you have rehearsals, reruns, angle shots and the lot. The wonderful thing about radio is how spontaneous it is. There's the microphone, there's the button – just go for it. I'm not saying there isn't a lot of research or preparation but it is much more natural as a form of communication, particularly talk radio.

'I was away for the shutdowns of the pirate stations in Cork. I was also away for the radio licence application hearings and for the awarding of the franchises. I had thought that ERI would get it. They had the studio and all the infrastructure required. What they hadn't done was sort out their VAT and that was the nail in the coffin for their licence bid. The lads in *The Cork Examiner* basically waltzed in and hoovered up the licence.

'What Pat Casey, Peter Cluskey, Denis Reading and Brendan Mooney were proposing as a radio station hadn't a hope of lasting. And it didn't. It lasted about a year. I came from Dublin back to Radio South to do an afternoon drive show. That was a story in itself because I had signed two contracts for Capitol Radio and Radio South and suddenly I was stuck in the middle of a contract war between two radio stations. I was three months working in Dublin waiting for Cork to go on the air. I was waiting for the inevitable which was having to make up my mind about what I was doing.

'Then Capitol had a big splash in *The Evening Herald* about me returning to Ireland from Canada. They saw this in Cork and had a fit. I was taken off the air by Capitol and was sent down to Cork because they said it would end up in court otherwise.

'Radio South was a disaster from the point of view of programming or structure. You could hear anything at any time of the day. It had no sense of familiarity when you turned the radio station on. It was a bit of a mess. It never had a hope and it wasn't long before it got gobbled up by bigger people with deeper pockets. The downside to it was that when radio stations change ownership, so many people get sacked. The whole station was virtually cleaned out overnight and some really good jocks lost their jobs. It was terrible. The late, great Joe O'Reilly was literally scrapheaped overnight. It was all wrong.

'The pirates were a very male-dominated world but there were some very good women working in the newsroom side of things. There was Siobhan Walls, Emer Lucey and Cathy Dillon – they were all top-notch and super journalists. It's funny because it was the same in Dublin radio where women seemed to work on the news. I don't remember a lot of female jocks, though way back in 1978 I did work with Susan O'Connor, aka Susan James, on CBC and she was really, really good. I met my wife Paula in the pirates when she produced my talk show. I also worked with some very talented men in ERI such as John Creedon, Liam Quigley, Joe Reilly and Sean O'Sullivan.

'The key thing that people often forget about when talking about pirate radio was how FM helped transform audio quality almost overnight. With broadcasting on the FM band you got CD-like quality, better range with your transmitter and much simpler aerials. With FM you only needed an aerial that was a couple of feet high whereas with AM you needed an aerial that was hundreds of feet high to get a signal out. That changed things overnight and it made listening to radio a joy. It also meant that with more people listening, stations started paying attention to studios, equipment, outside broadcasts and the like. I think ERI were probably the station that cottoned on to that first.

'Now, in fairness, I should point out that ERI didn't pioneer the whole "outside broadcast" thing. Back in 1979/80, we were doing outside broadcasts at CCLR. I remember doing a big gig with Eric Faldo and Roger Blythe down in the Arcadia. There must have been 1,000 people or more at it and it was certainly one of the earliest pirate discos. There were lots of other things happening at that time including the roller disco craze.

'There's a magic about radio that has never diminished for me. I still jump out of bed in the morning and look forward to that day's show. I often say to myself: "I'm actually getting paid to do this – something I love. It is bizarre." It is hugely satisfying to see how well the show is received. It is highly researched, thought out and planned, although sometimes all the planning gets scrapped and it takes on a life of its own – driven by the listeners. We get a radio audience book every three months so you know exactly how you are doing. I can remember when there were just 12,000 people listening. My show went to over 100,000 people which is amazing.

'The radio industry is massive now and while the print media is struggling to keep up with the changing face of news delivery it's fair to say that radio is holding its own. That is some achievement when you think of the alternatives available now. But people listen now for an awful lot more than the music. Back in the 1970s and 1980s it was all about the music. While music is still important people are now talking on air more than ever, the more the world progresses and the busier it becomes the more important local issues seem to be. Of course we do national and internal stories as well but local is our key.

'We have a new audience too – a huge diaspora listening overseas. It took years to build up but you never lose sight of the fact that the radio programme is only ever as good as the listener – the person who will ring up and contribute to the show. I am so lucky in that I have some listeners with me for almost forty years and am still gaining new listeners all the time, so it's like one big extended family really.

'It was tough to get there. There was a huge amount of work involved and years of evolution. But I think talk radio is in a very good place in Ireland. Most of us are trying to get the balance right, to offset a lot of the negative content with positive stuff. Talk is the most competitive form of radio on the dial in Ireland today. Everybody puts their talk radio on at the same time. We are all doing mid-morning and we are all competing against one another for the talk audience. It is the hardest place to be.

'What gives me the edge is the local element. I can do stuff about Cork that RTÉ, Today FM, Newstalk or the others can't. I can get into Cork homes about Cork news and Cork stories faster and better than the national stations. That is a huge advantage. But it is the toughest place to be.

'Pirate radio in Cork put me on the road to such a rewarding career. I started out at an incredible time and worked alongside some remarkable people and together we had some wonderful times. There were definitely tough times when you didn't know if you would be paid or if you would have a job the following week, but by and large they were great times and I wouldn't change anything about them.

'We were pioneers in an industry that really didn't want us, but we persisted and our persistence changed the face of radio in Ireland forever. Nobody can ever take that from us. The great thing about the pirates was that you got the opportunity to learn on the job in a way that was better than any college could teach you. You don't really have that today, not to the same extent anyway, although my son Luke has worked in the pirates in the last couple of years – it must be in his blood!'

CHAPTER SEVEN

Henry Condon, aka Henry Owen, aka Alan Reid: 'To start off with, really, I'm one of the lucky ones in that I ended up working with some of my absolute heroes: people from BBC Radio 1, like Simon Bates, Kid Jensen and later on Gary Davis, not to mention Chris Evans years later. I was really lucky in that I worked with my heroes which is absolutely fantastic. It is a bit like the young lad who goes into the football club he supported and then ends up in the first team.'

'I am so happy and proud that this was part of my life. My first memory of pirate radio was CBC in Cork. I listened to it on a crackly old AM transistor radio and I'd listen to people like Don Walsh, who was known as Dave Porter, and people like Stevie Bolger. Mark Cagney was on the air back then as well.

'I just wanted to be part of the whole thing. My radio buddies, such as John Creedon, used to have this fictitious pirate radio station in my house in Emmet Place and we would record each other playing various tracks. We didn't have anything beyond a simple tape recorder. We called the fictitious station Cork Local Radio (CLR) and I was Happy Harry and John was Eric Hansen. The two of us would spend hours playing music, recording ourselves and listening back to how we introduced stuff.

'From my early teenage years I dreamed of nothing else except being on radio. Radio Luxembourg was a godsend for us and we knew all the DJs by name. It was incredible for me listening to Kid Jensen on Radio Luxembourg, and then being privileged to get to work with him in later life.

'The BBC Top Twenty on a Sunday was part and parcel of our week. I couldn't get enough of it. This was what I wanted to do and, after listening to CBC in Cork, I decided I wanted to be part of it.

'By the summer of 1978 I had gotten involved in CBC and was presenting two weekend shows as Alan Reid. We were broadcasting from a basement on St Patrick's Hill, near the Wellington Road junction. My earliest memory of broadcasting at the time was being really, really nervous before my first show on a Saturday afternoon.

'My first record was a really, really cheesy Euro disco hit. I loved the sound of it and it was a big hit at the time. I stayed at CBC up until they moved away from St Patrick's Hill down to Penrose Quay. The studio was right beside Brian Boru Bridge in an old timber company office. I felt so cool in that studio because they were offices with glass partitions and it was almost like a real radio studio. Mind you, the soundproofing was absolutely rubbish.

'There was no such thing as broadcasting courses at the time. You learned by trial and error and by listening to how the really good DJs worked. That is how John Creedon and myself learned with our made-up CLR station. We learned by listening to radio, that's the truth of it. In fact, I don't think people who want to work in radio today do enough of that – they don't listen to enough radio to decide for themselves what they like, what they don't like and what they could do differently.

'We were constantly listening to different DJs, trying out different styles of presentation and regularly changing our favourite DJs. One day you would think Mike Reid was the coolest DJ in the business, the next it would be Bob Stewart from Radio Luxembourg. Remember that there was no pop radio station per se in Ireland at the time in the late 1970s. If you liked pop music at the time you had Larry Gogan on RTÉ and that was about it.

'It was an incredible period music-wise from 1974 to about 1980. You had such a huge variety of great music from the huge rock scene, the great soul stuff, disco and then punk. I suppose it was the disco sound that came to personify the era and, being honest, I absolutely loved it. In my opinion that era was simply the greatest with the whole soul sound merging into disco.

'Elton John had a big hit a few years back with "Are You Ready" and of course that was originally a hit for The Philadelphia Sound – it was great soul music and something I loved being part of and immersing myself in. Being a DJ on radio at that time was really exciting.

'It was the music made it exciting because a typical pirate radio station studio didn't amount to much. If you were really lucky there was a six-channel mixer. There was nothing like a mixing desk at that time. You'd have two decks and they were usually pretty basic. They certainly weren't Technic desks or anything like that. You worked with what was a disco deck pretty similar to what DJs were using in clubs at the time. That level of equipment didn't come in until the super pirates emerged in Cork in the mid to late 1980s.

'Pirate radio station studios in the 1970s were basically like discos except that you had broadcasting equipment linked in. For instance, on some of the tape decks you had to spool back the tape with your finger until you were exactly at the point you wanted.

85

'From the very beginning I believed that it was really important for a station to have its own "sound". That got me into the whole area of formats for radio. I felt it was really important that a station had its sound, that it was identifiable and distinct right through to the jingles that it used. How certain songs fitted the station's profile – it was a really important thing for me at the time. That's where my career was based in later years. When I later went to the United States I realised just how important formats were for a station.

'It basically involves how different radio stations should be doing different things to serve different segments of the audience. For instance, I think CBC had a real personality as a pirate station in the 1970s. CCLR came very quickly after CBC, first as Radio Shandon from Perry Street in Cork. Radio Shandon then became CCLR on French Church Street. It was also an important station in Cork.

'SouthCoast came much later and it became a super pirate station. It didn't launch until 1981, out of the Metropole Hotel. It came under pressure from RTÉ and, after The Metropole got some flak for having a pirate station on its premises, SouthCoast had to move out.

'Seeing the set-up at SouthCoast after being involved with CBC, CCLR and Radio City was a real eye-opener. It was Cork's first proper, fully kitted-and-booted pirate radio station. It was a super pirate and ERI came along pretty soon afterwards. It certainly upped the bar in terms of what could be done.

'I had been doing graphic design in the School of Art in Cork and I did the original logo for Radio City. Those stations had us doing a bit of everything. But SouthCoast and ERI brought in resources, equipment and an element of specialisation.

'The 1980s were a really tough time and I think that helped bring in a wide range of characters to the pirate stations that were around. Radio offered opportunities for people to get work and earn some cash. Not so much from the radio station but from the work that it generated such as being a DJ at various clubs.

'Getting involved back in the 1970s was a really important grounding for me. It was a great place to learn. You basically got to try everything in the station. So you learned from the ground up. By the end of 1984 I had moved to Radio Nova in Dublin which was a really professional set-up. I worked with household names of today in Radio Nova – people like Colm Hayes and John Carr and a whole bunch of others.

'It was a big move for me and I was happy to make it. But the reason I could make the move was because I had learned so much in the various Cork pirates. By the end of 1984 I was living in Chris Carey's house in Rathfarnham with his wife, Remi, and his children, Kirsty and Alex. Chris would come back every weekend from his other life in the UK – he had gotten involved in satellite receiver manufacturing. I remember sitting with Chris and talking about where our various industries were going.

'Chris was great because he was so passionate. One weekend he'd be talking about Kiss FM in Los Angeles and then the great "Boss" DJs in the States, guys like Charlie van Dyke. He was a great guy to spend time with because I learned so much about what was going on outside of Ireland.

'I look back now and realise how privileged I was to spend time with guys like that. After Radio Nova I moved on to another super pirate station in Dublin – they were almost all super pirates by this stage – called Q102FM and did afternoon slots for them. My first "real" and legal job in radio was with Radio City in Liverpool, after the pirate stations were closed down in 1989 by then-minister Ray Burke. I worked there for about a year and came back to work with Atlantic 252FM.

'The Liverpool move came about because a guy I knew, Tony MacKenzie, was working on-off with Radio City and he invited me over. That was it – I loved my time in Liverpool and it was a great grounding in the world of legal UK radio. But the Atlantic 252FM offer was very exciting and was too good to turn down. I was one of the first broadcasters they signed and I presented the first full show on the station from 9 a.m. to 11.30 a.m. By then I was Henry Owens.

'I was a personified Top 40 DJ – I believed that less was more. I was the kind of jock that firmly believed in more music and less talk. That was my style and what I loved. Timing was absolutely everything. I wanted to be able to say in 15 seconds what another DJ would take a couple of minutes to rattle off. That was my style.

'I never thought too far into the future. I wanted to make my living from radio and suddenly here I was doing exactly that. We were young and carefree and I don't think any of us were too pushed about money – we obviously liked having a few pound but it wasn't the be-all and end-all for us. In those times, there were very few options if you wanted to work on radio. If you wanted to work in legal radio and couldn't get a job in RTÉ you had no option but to move away and get a job with one of the UK stations.

'We worked in radio because we absolutely loved it. We did it because we wanted to be David Hamilton or Tony Prince. Later in my time with Atlantic 252FM I realised we were owned by the same firm that owned Radio Luxembourg. I not only got to go to Radio Luxembourg but I also spent time working there. I was in the same building from which the music that I had spent my teenage years listening to was broadcast.

'Some of the greats of the industry came from Radio Luxembourg and here was I, a young fella from Cork, working alongside them. Of course Chris Carey came from Radio Luxembourg and he was both Spangles Muldoon and Chris Carey on the station. In the 1990s, I was spending a lot of time in the UK for Atlantic 252FM. Then I moved full-time to the UK to be manager of Galaxy 102FM in Manchester around 1997. I helped with the launch of what was a legendary dance band – Galaxy is now looked back on as an important radio band.

'I stayed there for a couple of years and then the opportunity came along to be programme director of Virgin Radio in the UK. I got to work with people like Danny Baker, Jonathan Ross, Chris Evans, Gary Davis and Russ Williams. I had a fantastic time doing that. I never thought I'd leave but then the chance came along to help with the launch of RedFM back in Cork.

'I was part of the original licence. I was an original investor – in fact, I was the largest private investor in the station. I was chief executive when it launched in 2002. I stayed there until the end of 2005. But another opportunity came along in 2006 in Northern Ireland and I went for it. I was programme director of CoolFM and Downtown Radio for three years.

'I've had a great life – radio has been really, really good to me. It has been a privilege to have fallen in love with radio as a boy, be a fan of radio as a teen and then grow up to have a career in the industry as a man. I've worked alongside my heroes and some of the true greats of the industry. To me that is unbelievable. It is like the young Manchester United fan who gets to play for the club at Old Trafford and gets the ball passed to him by Ryan Giggs before scoring a goal. It's amazing.

'My first love was broadcasting but programming was the thing that got me into the management side of radio. I loved that too. To get to run a station like Galaxy or RedFm was a dream come true. Radio has changed totally since the 1970s in Ireland and there is some very exciting broadcasting today. For a country of its size, Ireland has an incredible amount of content available in radio.

'There is great radio in Ireland but, like everything else worldwide, there is also rubbish radio. But, by and large, radio in Ireland is in a very healthy state. In fact, much more so than in the UK where radio is now facing into very tough times. Radio in Cork, for instance, is very strong today between 96FM, RedFM and 103FM. Dublin also has some great stations.

'Irish people love to talk so it shouldn't be any surprise that talk radio here is so good – the content is excellent. But things change. In my day we wanted to be Kid Jensen or David Hamilton. Today young DJs want to be Fat Boy Slim or David Guetta. It's a totally different world out there. Youngsters have a different agenda to what we had and that's healthy because it is a different era.

'The problem is that youngsters today don't have the same kind of radio school that we had with the pirate stations. We could learn from our mistakes. We just wanted to be involved in broadcasting so you learned a little bit of everything. But youngsters today seem to want to be DJs and that's it. They don't have a place to mess about, learn the ropes and be given space to learn from their mistakes.'

CHAPTER EIGHT
The Clubs

They boasted exotic names like 'The Carousel', 'Good Time Charlies', 'Pharoahs', 'Cocos', 'Chandras'. 'Merlins', 'Mr Blueskies', 'Caesars', 'Krojacks', 'Papillon' and 'Snoopys'. They also boasted even more exotic-sounding DJs who were billed more for their pirate radio names than their actual identities.

But the Cork disco and club scene which emerged in the late 1970s was absolutely central to the development and eventual success of pirate radio on Leeside. 'Without discos and nightclubs there simply wouldn't have been any pirate radio stations,' TV3's Paul Byrne explained: 'For most DJs, it was the money we earned from playing discos and clubs that helped fund our early radio work. Most of us worked in radio for the pure love of it. You didn't get a penny, certainly not at the start. You depended on other jobs to pay the bills.'

Discos and nightclubs first emerged in Ireland in the very late 1960s and mirrored what was happening in the UK and United States. Ultimately, discos and nightclubs did to the dance halls what they had in turn done to the formal Irish orchestra dances in the 1950s. For decades, such orchestra dances had dominated the Irish social scene. However, by the early 1950s the dance halls and the showbands had emerged and, almost overnight, put paid to their strait-laced predecessors. For almost twenty years, show bands had ruled the roost in Ireland and became an entertainment cash machine the likes of which the country had never seen before.

They produced such entertainment giants as The Royal Showband, The Dixies, The Capitol, Joe Dolan, Dickie Rock, The Miami, The Cadets and a host of others. In Ireland, these bands were the equivalent, in their day, of Elvis Presley in the US and The Beatles across the Irish Sea.

Venues sprouted up all around Ireland with such famous names in Cork as 'The Majestic', 'The Top Hat', 'Palm Court', 'Hill Top,' 'The Arcadia' and 'The Stardust'. For two decades ballrooms essentially had licenses to print money. Dancehall owners and promoters coined it as thousands flocked to dances – and the funds generated became so lucrative that even parish priests and parish councils got in on the act and organised their own dances.

Fans queued for admission and the hysteria that greeted the acts meant the bands became Ireland's first entertainment superstars, rivalling the newly emerged stars of Radio Éireann such as Gay Byrne, Mike Murphy, Bunny Carr and Frankie Byrne.

It has only been in recent years that the true impact of the showband era has been reassessed as the remarkable phenomenon it was. The acts involved weren't just household names in Ireland – they became major stars in Europe and the United States. It became one of the great musical quirks of fate that The Beatles once played support to The Royal Showband during one of their UK performances.

However, in the mid 1960s, the showband era slowly but inexorably began to slide into decline. The major Irish acts began to find it more lucrative to work overseas. The Royal Showband took up a money-spinning residency in Las Vegas and things were never quite the same. The ballrooms on which the showbands depended simply weren't able to compete with the new entertainment venues which younger generations increasingly favoured. The first sign of trouble was when early and midweek dances, once guaranteed sell-outs, slowly became to be phased out due to dwindling numbers.

'It was very much as if the ballrooms were for the parents and the new discos, nightclubs and lounge bars were for the youngsters coming up in the late 1960s and 1970s,' the late former Taoiseach and ballroom impresario Albert Reynolds once explained. 'The country music scene was still there but the days of people queuing for hours just to get into a dancehall were over.'

Alcohol was one factor in the transformation. Whereas most ballrooms were 'dry', discos were usually in hotels where drink sales were a vital part of the business. The evolution of better sound systems also swung the balance towards discos. Youngsters suddenly questioned why they should pay to listen to Irish bands play covers of their favourite hit songs from the UK and the US, sometimes of fairly mediocre quality, when they could listen to the real thing in excellent sound quality in a disco.

Other key factors were that discos and nightclubs often undercut the admission fees for ballrooms as their overheads were substantially lower. They depended on recorded music and a good DJ, whereas a ballroom owner had to pay a full band, sometimes of up to eight members strong.

But, perhaps most important of all, slowly but inexorably the rock venues, discos and nightclubs came to be seen as 'cooler' than the ballrooms of the 1950s and 1960s. It helped that they were heavily featured in most films coming from the

US and UK, a factor that only made them seem more modern than the dated ballrooms and dancehalls. They reflected what was happening in New York, San Francisco, London and Paris at the current time. In contrast, the ballrooms seemed to hark back to a post-World War II era.

'The dancehalls found themselves faced by the live rock concert on the one hand and the disco and club scene on the other. If you wanted to dance, you went to a disco or a nightclub. If you wanted to listen to music, you went to a rock concert. The old showbands were caught between a rock and a hard place,' Mr Reynolds added.

The showband scene never fully disappeared. It morphed into the current Irish country music scene and, in places, ballrooms continued to ply their trade well into the 1990s, with venues such as Maudie Macs outside Mallow being a prime example. But, from the early 1970s on, it was the disco and nightclub that increasingly dominated the Irish entertainment scene.

Author Vincent Power recounted in his bestselling book, *Send 'Em Home Sweatin*, that the emergence of discos and nightclubs cast the old ballrooms into a negative light from which they are only now emerging. He wrote that it was sad how the key role they played in Ireland's social development was largely ignored until recent years: 'Showbands played a central role in Ireland's cultural and musical development, a role largely unacknowledged.

'For all their mediocrity and imitation, they laid the foundation for Irish pop voices of the future. The success of bands like U2, The Corrs and The Cranberries is rooted not only in the development of Irish rock by the likes of Thin Lizzy, Skid Row, Taste and Horslips. To chart the history of Irish pop and ignore the showband factor would be a travesty,' he wrote.

However, it is worth noting that it was only with the decline of the old ballrooms and the emergence of nightclubs and discos that Irish pirate radio began to emerge. RedFM's Neil Prendeville, aka Jim Lockhart, said that discos and nightclubs were part and parcel of the whole pirate radio industry.

'It was an 11 p.m. to 4 a.m. gig – but it paid big money, around IR£30. Some people weren't earning that in a week. It was great – all your music was supplied and all you had to do was turn up. This led to more gigs and pretty soon with the combination of the radio work I realised I could be onto a career path.'

The Carousel was the first of its kind in Cork. It was run by Jim Dillon and gave Cork a taste of what disco was like. It also brought overseas DJs into Cork and, for the first time, youngsters who were listening to BBC Radio 1, Radio Caroline and Radio Luxembourg experienced music at first hand that they simply weren't hearing on RTÉ. Stevie Bolger recalled that one of the stars of The Carousel was a DJ named "The Beast" – a UK operator called Phil McQueen who earned the title through his sheer physical size.

'That was an incredible place – it was like nothing Cork had ever seen before. It wasn't long before a host of other clubs started to sprout up around the city. I came to Cork to work at a place called Good Time Charlies. For a time, that was the place to go in the city. But the club scene was always changing and new places were always opening up.'

Another DJ, Dan Noonan, aka Karl Johnson, recalled the slow but steady emergence of the nightclub industry. 'When I started out in the 1970s there were actually very few dedicated nightclubs around the place. The main one was Krojaks. We used to gig mostly in the hotels like the Country Club, the Silversprings with Papillon, Vienna Woods with Snoopys and then the rugby clubs like Cork Con, Highfield and the others like the Shandon Boat Club.

'The scene did progress from that and I suppose pirate radio had a role in it. I used to buy all my records in Ursula's Record Store on Oliver Plunkett Street and it was there that I heard CBC for the first time. I was working as a DJ on the club circuit. I bought my first set of gear from DJ Daniels and we were all taken with the new station. In fact, Terry Shannon, who would go on to serve as Lord Mayor of Cork, worked in Ursula's for a time.

'I suppose it was only a matter of time before I asked the great DJ Daniels for a slot. It took me about nine months working as a DJ before I did my first stint on radio. I was only seventeen and I suppose radio was the next step for a DJ. It was like being a mobile DJ and having a slot on pirate radio suddenly became very important for landing the better DJ gigs.

'At the time, the nightclubs were screaming for the DJs that worked for 2FM. But CBC, in my opinion, was on a par with the Dublin stations in terms of the quality of the presenters. It was a classy operation. It's funny really but CBC was operating from a basement up on St Patrick's Hill and I think the premises later went to Alcoholics Anonymous.

'The number of people that listened to pirate radio was unbelievable. You'd do a CBC gig in The Country Club on a Monday night and you could have 400 people there – and the DJ was in his teens! It was amazing stuff. It's hard to believe but I am still working off the name that I earned back then as a DJ. People still come up to me and say: "Ah, it's you Karl Johnson – I remember you from CBC or one of the other pirates." I don't think any of us realised at the time precisely what we had.'

The dynamic of the Cork nightclubs and pirate radio stations was quite unique. UK-born DJ Nick Richards, who moved to Cork and now anchors 96FM's early morning slot, admitted he was hugely impressed by the quality of local broadcasting. 'I wanted to get into radio. I drifted around city jobs in the UK and I went into a newsagent's and found a magazine called *DJ & Radio Monthly*. It lasted for about twenty issues but it was all about the radio industry at the time. It just hooked me straight away – there was stuff about the Radio Luxembourg DJs, the guys on BBC and the DJs on Radio Caroline.

'There were also a few pages about pirate radio and those were the pages I kept coming back to. As it so happened, a few years later I went out and worked on the Radio Caroline ship. I decided I wanted to do radio and it was really hard to break into the industry in the UK. When Radio Caroline came back on the air, about twenty miles out to the open sea, it lived a charmed life for a few years. It was a big adventure for me but the ship was in a really poor condition. You did everything from checking generators to pumping fuel, to cleaning, painting and then helping with broadcasts.

'By the time the Radio Caroline ship had finally sunk, I had heard there were pirate radio stations starting up in Cork and that's why I travelled over with a one-way ticket. Being able to say I worked on Radio Caroline really opened a few doors for me here. But I was totally taken aback by the quality of the DJs. The standard in the clubs and pirate stations here was really, really high.'

In some cases in Cork, the early nightclubs and discos simply supplanted the old ballrooms. For instance, The Palm Court on Oliver Plunkett Street was transformed into a nightclub called Good Time Charlies in the early 1970s. For a time, it was the trendiest and most popular venue in Cork city. It was reinvented again as Zoes in the 1980s. It was later rebuilt and became first Scotts bar and restaurant before its latest incarnation as The Oliver Plunkett in the 2000s.

Hotels were key drivers in the transformation in the 1970s and profit was the fuel for change. A successful disco was correctly identified as a goldmine for hoteliers. It was a cash business with a huge spin-off trade in drink and food sales. Hence it was no surprise that, from the late 1970s, discos began to open in droves. The Hotel Blarney had Pharoahs, The Grand Hotel in Fermoy had Caesars and The Victoria Hotel had the legendary Cocos. Jury's had The No-Name Club and Blackrock Castle had Merlins.

The Grand Parade Hotel for a decade came to dominate the Cork city centre disco scene with first Stardust and then the legendary Chandras. The latter proved a starting point for dozens of the DJs who would go on to become household names, not just in Cork but in Ireland. Decades after it closed, Chandras remains a popular topic of conversation on social media and one of the reference points for the whole Cork disco scene.

By the early 1980s the Cork nightclub scene had been joined by such venues as Spiders, Redz, Fast Eddies, The Pav, Porkys, Mangans and Swingers. Even halls and community centres got in on the act with St Francis Hall offering Mr Blueskies Disco.

Live acts revolved around two legendary Cork venues, Sir Henry's and De Lacy House. 'The Blackpool Sentinel' blog authoritatively argued that neither venue ever got the credit they deserved for the live music scene they supported and encouraged in Cork in the 1980s and 1990s.

'I've long thought that De Lacy House never really received the credit it deserved as an excellent live music venue, especially between 1988 and 1994. Against the long-established might of Sir Henry's, it was at a reputational disadvantage from the off, but promoters like Jim Walsh, the late Des Blair and the other Denis Desmond worked Don Forde's top floor hard and with no little sense of adventure,' The Sentinel argued.

'Far from rivalling Sir Henry's, De Lacy's complimented it instead, often presenting a far more diverse range of output, reaching across a broad spectrum, from folk and trad to out-and-out indie. And this may indeed have been a weakness as much as it was a strength – one could, quite literally, see anything there.'

It is now a matter of musical pride for Cork fans to claim to have been present at either venue for gigs by such emerging but as yet unheralded bands as Nirvana, Five Guys Named Moe, U2, Aslan, Something Happens, The Pogues, Thin Lizzy, Cry Before Dawn and a galaxy of others.

Sir Henry's opened in 1978, named after the baker, Henry O'Shea, who operated an historic premises on South Main Street. It lasted for twenty-five glorious years and its undoubted claim to fame came on 20 August 1991, when it hosted a band called Sonic Youth. They were supported by a little-known group from Seattle in the US – Kurt Cobain's Nirvana. Less than twelve months later, Nirvana would be the hottest rock group on the planet. Tragically, Cobain would take his own life in April 1994 aged just twenty-seven.

For a venue capable of only holding a couple of hundred, even after its small kitchen was closed to allow for an expansion of facilities, there are now over 10,000 people in Cork who claim to have been in Sir Henry's that famous night to see Kurt Cobain and Nirvana.

Such was the impact Sir Henry's had on the Cork social scene that, eleven years after the venue closed its doors for the last time, University College Cork (UCC) staged a special exhibition on its legacy. The exhibition, staged over the summer of 2014, was organised by Eileen Hogan of UCC's School of Applied Social Studies, DJ Stevie Grainger, aka Stevie G, and Martin O'Connor of the UCC Library.

'Oral histories were collected and formed part of the exhibition and part of the archive. Written guest posts about people's memories of Sir Henry's were also collected. These stories provided a rare insight into the lived experience of Sir Henry's from the perspective of key actors in the scene. The inclusion of these histories documents these memories for posterity,' Ms Hogan said.

'The exhibition illuminated in a fun and accessible way a sense of what Sir Henry's was like and why it was significant to the people of Cork and beyond. In short, its emotional, aesthetic, musical, cultural and historical value and legacy.'

Not surprisingly, such live rock and disco venues became a legendary part of the Cork social scene. When the great Liverpool side of the 1980s visited Cork to play a friendly against a League of Ireland XI, they partied after the match in Cocos. One of the hilarious stories to emerge involved a club DJ and Kenny Dalglish who had a ten-minute conversation before parting company. Both later admitted to their friends that neither had a clue what the other had said – the DJ unable to understand Dalglish's thick Glasgow accent and the Scottish striker unable to comprehend the Leeside vernacular.

Tony Whitnell, aka Tony Clarke, aka DJ Top Cat, was part of the Cork scene from the 1970s. Tony started with CBC/ABC and quickly became one of the most popular DJs in Cork: 'I was around eighteen when I started in the business and I stuck with it until my late twenties. I worked with Capitol Radio and ERI later on. It was an amazing time really. There was fantastic music around. My father worked in The Pavilion Cinema so he got a lot of albums for free which were to be played before films. So I got a great record collection which was a big thing back then if you were a DJ.

'But the music being produced was really top class, particularly in terms of dance music. You had Donna Summer, Rod Stewart, Abba and the whole disco thing. I liked music across the whole spectrum from the Rat Pack right through to rock and country. But the discos emerged at a time when dance music was really, really strong. It was no surprise that the discos did so well in Cork.'

Tony never went full-time as a DJ – something he still has mixed feelings about. 'I was one of those that had a really good job. I was working in Sunbeam, I was on pretty good money and eventually I became part of the management team out there. I never had the bottle to go for it full-time. After eleven years at that I went working for myself. I loved the whole DJ thing as a part-time gig. I used to leave work at 4.30 p.m. and a fella called Pat Busteed used to take me from Sunbeam across to 'The Country Club' and I was on the radio at 5 p.m. I was on until 7 p.m. It was a fantastic scene and I even gave up sport for it.

'I would have loved to have gone full-time but it was so volatile. I had a mortgage in my twenties and I just didn't want to take the chance. There was no job security in it back then. I had a young family and I didn't really want to take the risk. But the fun in the stations and nightclubs was incredible. Those years were amongst the highlights of my life – it was a great, great time in Cork.'

However, just as economic factors caught up with Cork's pirate radio stations, so too the famous nightclubs began to fall victim to changing trends and fashions. The Pav was opened in the 1990s by promoter Kenny Lee and quickly became the most popular venue in the city. But it had vanished in less than a decade. Similarly, Sidetracks opened in the 1990s and for more than a decade it became one of Cork's busiest venues. Then it too fell victim to changing tastes. The new arrivals included Havana Browns, The Roxy, The Bodega, The Bowery, Voodoo Rooms, The Hanover – Cubins and The Savoy (albeit revamped).

'It is almost as if each place has its own lifespan,' former DJ, pirate radio host and award-winning *Evening Echo* photographer Eddie O'Hare explained: 'A new venue opens, it becomes the place to go and then, over time, it either gets new rivals or it loses that sense of magic it opened with. Some venues spend a lot of money reinventing themselves and they are the ones that seem to last longest.

'The other factor is that there is a lot more competition today for late night entertainment than there was back in the 1970s and 1980s. You have live soccer on TV, you have evening rugby games under floodlights, you have comedy clubs which were unheard of thirty years ago and you have special late night bars. I'd say there is four or five times more competition today for evening entertainment than there was back in the 1970s and 1980s. In a way it was a bit of a captive market back then.

'Today, clubs are still doing well but I think they have to fight a lot harder for business. I know people have a lot more money to spend than we did back then, but I still think that people have so many choices about where to go and what to do at night. In the 1970s the clubs and discos were really the only port of call. But that is part of what made it all so special.'

CHAPTER NINE

Trevor Welch, aka Scott Jensen, aka Trevor Stephens: 'My interest in the whole broadcasting scene started when I was in school. I was about eleven at the time. There were eight of us – six girls and two boys – and there was always music in the house.

'My mother did a bit of singing and the record player, a small Pioneer model, always seemed to be playing. My first record was Abba's "Does Your Mother Know" and I remember an old Rod Stewart record and the sound tapping out from it. Music and sport were my life at the time.

'I loved soccer and if I wasn't out playing it, I was out in the alley near our home, giving a running commentary on Manchester United's win in the 1977 FA Cup final against Liverpool.

'A neighbour, Paul O'Leary's dad, gave me a broken microphone one day and I thought I was the bee's knees with that. I was always doing mock commentaries. But the big step for me was going to Deerpark school and then rushing home to hear my brother Noel on CBC radio. I thought CBC was like a fairytale. It was on our doorstep and RTÉ didn't seem to be doing much of Cork interest.'

'From there I discovered Radio Luxembourg and the BBC. But they were pretty far away and CBC had this wonderful local resonance. It arrived around 1978 at the same time as I was doing mock commentaries on Manchester United and Liverpool.

'I was so proud that my brother was on the radio. He went by the handle Noel Evans. I used to go into Deerpark and tell everyone my brother was on CBC. They couldn't believe it. It was the coolest thing ever. I remember rushing home to listen and pretend to be on the radio myself.

'It wasn't long before I was annoying the shit out of everyone about broadcasting, working on radio and being a DJ. I remember Noel came home with this Ford Capri car. It was a white car that had a black roof and was covered in CBC stickers. Noel was heading out to do discos with bags of records. I thought it was the coolest thing I'd ever seen.

'As a young fella, my world now revolved around sport and music. I had no interest in anything else. My No. 1 goal was to play professional football but I never managed to reach that level. I played Munster Senior League with Wembley – that was as good as it got for me. So it was inevitable that my next step would be a career in radio or TV.

'The breakthrough for me came when I started to practice being a DJ with advice from Noel. My diction wasn't there at the start but I worked very hard, I taped myself and listened back to what I was doing. I was brave enough, by 1983, when I was seventeen, to cycle down to the Radio Caroline caravan in Togher and ask if I might do a bit for them. Mickey Daly answered the door, all long hair and attitude, like a rocker from Status Quo, and I said I wanted to have a go on air.

'I was listening to guys like Don Hynes, aka Donal McKeown, and Ken Tobin, our neighbour, who used to call himself Steve Davis. There was also Paul Byrne, PJ Coogan and Rob Allen.'

'I handed in a tape to Mickey and said I wanted to do anything that was available. He called me back and said they had a show on a Saturday which was after Donie McKeown. Myself and Ken Tobin worked on the slot and the show was called "Hit or Miss". It was all about the pop charts and which songs were likely to be a hit and which were likely to sink without trace.

'I always remember the song "The Power of Love" by Frankie Goes To Hollywood. It was released and I remember the excitement on the show of saying to listeners that this was going to be a massive hit. I predicted that it was a definite No. 1 coming up to Christmas. Ken Tobin disagreed with me and said it was going to be a flop. I've been slagging him about it ever since.

'I think I was going by the name Scott Jensen at the time. My friend, Jimmy McGrath, was huge into making up names. He had a vivid imagination and he was more excited than I was at the prospect of coming up with a "handle" that I'd use on air. There was a guy on BBC Radio 1 called Kid Jensen and that's where Jimmy came up with Scott Jensen. It was a bit far out but that was the start for me.

'I was working at the time in John O'Mahony's bookmakers. I'd also done a paper round for Dawson's around Glasheen and Wilton. I saved all my money and then went to O'Mahony's. Every penny I had from 1982 onwards was spent on music. I couldn't pass a record shop without going in to buy the latest singles or albums. Back then you had to build up your own collection because no DJ was going to lend you his collection for fear it would get damaged or lost.

'Radio Caroline was a great place to start. There was a fantastic atmosphere and Mickey Daly was a great guy to work with. I will never forget his mother, God rest her, calling out to the caravan every day with the tea and biscuits for whoever was on air. That's the kind of place it was.

'You built your skills and your confidence. From there, Mick O'Brien, God rest him, took over SouthCoast Radio. I knew Mick from the scouts and from refereeing football matches and that's where the contact came from. This was probably the third coming of SouthCoast. I told Mickey Daley I was going to SouthCoast and he wasn't best pleased. It felt a bit like jumping ship but it was time to move on.

'Mick O'Brien had heard me on Radio Caroline and told me to call in to the SouthCoast offices off North Main Street back around 1985. I decided to change my "handle" from Scott Jensen to Trevor Stevens. It was easier working with my own first name and the Stevens bit came from a really good footballer with Howard Kendall's Everton at the time.

'My first big gig with them was down at the Shandon Boat Club on a Saturday night. "Porky's Nightclub" was one of the popular haunts in Cork at the time. It was on the River Lee right by Pairc Uí Chaoimh. I went with my buddies and knew I was on the late shift from midnight until around 3 a.m. I left the nightclub around 10.30 p.m. and got a taxi into town. I was shaking with nerves. The SouthCoast offices were up over the Kentucky Fried Chicken premises and I remember going in and the first record I played was Electric Light Orchestra's "Mr Blue Sky". That night was a major step up for me.

'A lot of the SouthCoast presentation at the time was inherited from the previous SouthCoast operation. Things like the "jingles" were all pretty much carried over. Bob Stokes, a Dublin guy who was on with us at the time, could do incredible things with his voice – his voice was basically like an instrument. He did the effects like howling winds or a Dracula-style voice to introduce late night shows. There was no money to do anything else – I remember him doing a voice through a Wavin pipe one day to try and get the effect right.

'It was a big challenge but we got by. I remember John Caulfield, now Cork City's manager, had started playing Munster Senior League with us at Wembley and he used to call in to SouthCoast to see me. It was a cool kind of thing to be hanging out in a pirate radio station. He'd even help me pick out the music. But sport and music used to go hand in hand because, thanks to my job in O'Mahony's, I'd have the list of all the day's winners from whatever horse racing meeting was on and I'd read them out as part of the sports bulletin on SouthCoast. It used to go down a treat.

'To be honest, it was a magic time in Cork. There was a lot of respect for what the pirate stations were doing and there was a fantastic Irish music scene. I remember U2 playing "Lark by the Lee" but I couldn't make it because I was a sub for Wembley in a cup final against Waterford. We lost 3–0 and I missed U2. I'm a U2 fanatic so you can imagine how I felt that evening.

'I think what made pirate radio in Cork so special at the time was the characters involved. Fergal Barry was straight out of school and was reading news for us, a bit like the Nutty Professor. Paul Byrne loved to have a joke on radio and when Fergal was trying to read the news, Paul was shoving ice cubes down the back of his shirt. Another time he set fire to a bin in the studio and the entire place was full of smoke while we were trying to keep things going on air. He used to drive station manager Mick O'Brien absolutely mad.

'But we all became great friends and even now, thirty years later, we are all still the very best of mates. SouthCoast wasn't just a place we worked – it was almost like a community, a place where we went to socialise and chat. Even when we weren't broadcasting ourselves we would still call in to see the lads or listen to their programme in the studio.

'At times it was like a party atmosphere in there although I'm sure poor Mick O'Brien was almost driven to tears by the whole thing. He was a very professional guy and very serious about what he was doing. He even compiled a special "Do Not Play" list – songs such as Madonna's "Like A Virgin". Mick was very religious and didn't want to offend what he saw as conservative Cork listeners. But Paul was on one evening and played all five songs on the banned list back-to-back. Mick almost crashed his car driving in to the studio to find out what had happened.

'In the commercial sense, I'd say the station was just about in the black. I don't think a lot of money was being made at that point. But there were definite signs of the money that could be made by the late 1980s when the prospect of licenses suddenly came into the picture. In the mid 1980s, we'd get maybe IR£10 or so on a Friday evening. We'd go to Maudie Whelan's for a few drinks after work and that IR£10 got us a long way. None of us were in it purely for the money, though all of us dreamed of making a living from radio or TV.

'I had a job so I was making a bit of money and could supplement what I was doing with SouthCoast. I was also doing a bit of DJ work as well. I was in De Lacy House and I was in Frankie's Bar. I wanted to keep at it because I honestly believed something would come out of it for me. I had a passion for it and I had a feeling that something might come my way in terms of the sports broadcasting side of things.

'There was a buzz from it. You'd be doing a disco and you'd

mention to someone that you did some radio work and straight away they'd ask: "Are you the Trevor Stevens on SouthCoast?" You'd get people looking for requests or asking your opinion about bands. But I'd reached the stage where I preferred radio work, more even though it paid an awful lot less than the DJ work in clubs. De Lacy House paid very well for work in the 1980s.

'John Fullam was a guy involved with SouthCoast. When SouthCoast closed down in 1988 he went to Galway and started up a station called Coast 103FM. Paul Byrne and myself went up there for the summer, while I applied for Cork Multichannel TV, which had started in 1985 and was hiring. This was 1988 and they were starting to dip their toes in the whole area of sport.

'I got a phone call to say that I'd an interview with Michael McNamara for Cork Multichannel. I was asked to do a bit of commentary. It was only fifteen minutes of a highlights match but, at the end of it, I was told the job was mine, but to cut my hair. I'd grown my hair long like Bono but it wasn't acceptable if I was going to be in front of the camera. That's where multichannel TV was born and that's how I shifted from radio to TV. But for years I wasn't sure that TV was me – I always thought I'd return to radio. Radio was such an immediate form of communication and I loved that aspect of it. In many ways it was an easier gig than TV.

'I remember talking to the late, great Don Weldon around 1990 and telling him how I missed radio. He told me TV was going well for me and to keep building my profile. He said to stick with TV and I took his advice. I persevered with it and eventually I was able to combine TV with radio. It is twenty-five years later and I'm still involved with TV.'

'But if you ask me, I'd probably say my best days, certainly the most enjoyable work days of my life, were all on SouthCoast back between 1985 and 1988. What was great about it at the time was that you could make a mistake on air and it wouldn't be career-ending, just so long as it wasn't too horrific. There was a famous one where one of the lads fell asleep on a graveyard shift and all you could hear was snoring from the studio and the sound of dogs barking in the background from North Main Street. It went on for over forty minutes until someone could get into the studio and wake him up.

'It was a once-in-a-lifetime place to work. We were all in it together and I don't think any of us worried about the fact the station was illegal. It was a win-win situation for me because I was doing something I loved. I had my work in O'Mahony's, then the DJ work and I was even doing MC for quiz nights for a while as an extra earner.

'I suppose people noticed the fact I loved the job. I was editing sport one day when John Lynch of RTÉ mentioned to me that TV3 were advertising for staff in preparation for going live as Ireland's first commercial television station in 1998. He told me: "Trevor, this is right down your alley – you have to go for it." I hadn't even seen the advertisement. My brother Noel helped me do up my CV and I sent it off. I had ten years' experience under my belt and that helped a lot.

'In May 1998 I had my first interview in Sandyford in Dublin with Bob Hughes, Andrew Hanlon and Kieran Devanney, who came from Sky. I got a second interview which was in Windmill Lane. Gráinne Seoige was sitting there beside me for the interviews and she was speaking fluent Irish down the phone to a friend of hers. I remember thinking I was in trouble because I hadn't anything more than a sentence of Irish. The funny part about the day was that I was more excited about being in the studio where U2 recorded their first album than the prospect of getting a dream job in sport with TV3.

'Bob Hughes called me the following day and asked me how I felt about being anchorman for TV3 Sport. It was brilliant – one of the best days of my life, but I was instantly so nervous that my stomach went to jelly, both at the prospect of the challenges of the new job and having to leave Cork. I'm a huge home bird and I'd never worked outside of Cork before. I knew it was a big step but one that I couldn't back away from.

'It opened up a new world for me in broadcasting. Just two years later TV3 got UEFA Champions League matches and suddenly I was commentating on games involving Manchester United, Real Madrid, AC Milan and Barcelona. It had been two and a half years since I commentated and my first match was in the Nou Camp between Barcelona and Leeds United. Barcelona won 4–0 and I was with John Toshack. It was a roasting day in Barcelona, I was wearing a white shirt and I was soaked in sweat from the heat and nerves before the match had even kicked off. But it was an unbelievable experience. I wasn't happy with how I did but the producer Michael Lynn said he was happy enough, though he felt there was room for improvement given that I'd been out of commentating for so long. But I learned so much that night. I got the tapes and went over them non-stop for the next few weeks. I never looked back and, fifteen years later, people are still coming to me asking for me to commentate on games.

'But it was all down to the basic skills I learned at SouthCoast as well as the discos and clubs around Cork. If you love what you do and take a bit of pride in it, you won't go far wrong. Where you grow up definitely shapes you. It's funny because Togher had a bad name. I suppose I could easily have gone down another road. A few friends of mine got into a lot of trouble over the years. But it was a wonderful place for me because of the fact that you had Radio Caroline and great guys like Mickey Daly. The people involved in sport out there were incredible too and it's important to remember that for every person who makes headlines for the wrong reasons there are four or five out there doing the right thing for their family, friends and neighbours.

'Togher doesn't really get the credit it deserves for all the great things happening out there. Look at the people that have come from Togher over the years – Denis Irwin, Brian Carey, Rob Heffernan and the famed St Finbarr's hurling and football Club. I know people that wouldn't say they were from Togher when they were going for a job and that hurt me because I was always proud of the place and the fact my life changed thanks to a radio station run from a caravan in the back garden of a Togher house.

'I got back into radio initially with RedFM in Cork in 2001/02. The station was starting up and Henry Condon rang me and asked me to do a sports show at the weekends. TV3 initially didn't like the idea but they allowed me to do it once they got a regular "plug". I think Henry wanted "a name" to do their sports programme because they were going to be competing with 96FM, who were so well established. I loved the idea of the show which was known as *Trevor Welch's Big Red Bench*. The reaction to it was great and we won a PPI award in 2002 for "Best Sports Programme". It was the year the Irish Open Golf was at Fota and the World Cup was on. We broadcast live from Fota and I was lucky enough to get some incredible interviews. I was really chuffed because we beat Today FM to the award, which was a huge thing for a regional station like ours.

'I'm glad to say that I continue to work on mainstream radio today, working on perhaps one of the favourite radio shows that I have ever presented, *The Score* on Cork's 96FM on Saturdays from 2–6 p.m. The show has the perfect balance of music and sport and I get to do interviews with local, national and international sports stars. As I say to people, it's hard to go wrong with a sports show in Cork. It's a two-man show which is produced by JP McNamara who is absolutely terrific at his job. It's a programme that started in February 2009 and is going stronger than ever today, thank God.

'There have been so many great memories for me on both radio and TV. I got to interview Sir Alex Ferguson five times. Every time I interviewed him Manchester United had won, so I was really lucky in that regard. He could be difficult and awkward when he wanted to be. But I found him an incredibly interesting guy and definitely the highest profile football person I have ever interviewed.

'Sometimes in your career you need a lucky break. That something will fall right for you. In 2010, Jose Mourinho came back to Stamford Bridge with Inter Milan and knocked out his old club Chelsea from the UEFA Champions League. It can sometimes be hit-and-miss with interviews. TV3 used to be fourth or fifth on the priority list for interviews and Mourinho had done three interviews already so I thought there was no way he was going to talk to us.

'But I waited and waited and we were going to be off air at 10.30 p.m. when I saw Jose coming down a corridor at 10.20 p.m. with custard cream biscuits in his pocket and he chewing away on them. We had three minutes and time for just two questions. You have to be daring at that level, so I stuck the microphone in front of him and said: "Well done, Jose, on your win tonight." But he said he was still chewing his custard creams. We got our two questions in and I thanked him and said I hoped he enjoyed his biscuits, literally a couple of seconds before we went off the air. It worked really, really well.

'When I look back now on my career as a whole, I am conscious that pirate radio was such an important schooling place for me. It shaped me really. When I hear music from the seventies and eighties being played on radio today it takes me back to a young Trevor Stevens arriving for his late night show at SouthCoast in the North Main Street studio. There was magic in the air back then. As U2 put it, it was "All That You Can't Leave Behind".

CHAPTER TEN

Paul Byrne, aka Paul Stevens, aka Paul Davis: 'I had a three-in-one stereo system and I remember listening to the radio in a room at home in Douglas in the late seventies or early eighties. I took an immediate interest in pirate radio. I don't know why but I thought to myself that I'd love to have a go at it.

'Looking back on it now, it is a bit embarrassing. I used to sit in front of the three-in-one and talk into a hairbrush and pretend it was a microphone. I just loved the idea of being a DJ. But when I recall all the people in pirate radio back then, a lot of them did something very similar because we loved the magic of radio and wanted to carve out a career. I suppose a stonemason will practice with stone, a painter will practice with paint – I wanted to work in radio and I was simply practising the skills I thought I'd need.

'To be honest, I always classed pirate radio as the FÁS of Irish broadcasting. It was the best stepping stone someone like me could have dreamed for. You could not have bought the education and training that we got as teenagers in the pirates. It was incredible because you were learning at the coalface. You weren't getting money but you were getting the skills to build a career.

'We all did it for the love of it. We all loved radio. And I think that is what made the whole thing so special – you had a bunch of people who cared about the music, the programmes and their audience. They weren't bothered about money or advertising.

'I can't explain it. I remember contacting CCLR at French Church Street in the city centre. I went in and was told that they needed a demo tape. I went to a friend's house and put together a proper demo. A week or two later I was offered a fifteen minute slot every Saturday morning.

'It was for a show called *Teen Beat* and I almost shit myself before I went on air all that week. My late father, God rest him, scripted the entire fifteen minutes for me. He said I could pick out the music myself but that he would help me with the script. I will always remember that. My first broadcast words were, and I will never forget them: "Good morning everybody, welcome to Teen Beat, I am Paul Byrne and I will be with you now, from the hour of eleven until the hour of eleven fifteen." Those words will stay with me until the day I die.

'I then said: "OK, teen beaters, let's wake you up on this Saturday morning ..." I remember pressing the button and I played Michael Jackson's "One Day In Your Life". I came home and I asked my Dad what he thought? He asked me how I could have played such a ridiculously slow song at the start of a radio programme. He said it would turn people off. My Dad was involved in entertainment and he was right. That song almost cost me my career before I'd even started.

'But it was all about learning. I never again started a show with such a slow song. I did fifteen minutes every Saturday morning for months to come and, about four months later I got a really big break: I was offered thirty minutes! I had just turned fifteen and was still in secondary school. Radio became like an addiction for me.'

'I remember being in school from Monday to Friday and all I could think about was my fifteen minute show on Saturday.

All I wanted to do was work on radio. I despised every single waking minute of the day that I was in class. If we had a break at 11 a.m., which you do quite often in school, I used to actually run from my school, which was five minutes from CCLR, down to the station and sit inside in the studio to listen to the DJ that was on air. There was something about radio that I loved.

'I don't think it was the music. It was more the fascination of radio and the way it worked and wove itself into people's lives. You were broadcasting from what could only be described as a pigsty. It was a room, two bad partitions and there was a constant smell of drink and tobacco. At the time, most pirates were located near pubs or clubs and guys were always bringing drink into work with them.

'I think everyone smoked at the time and, as a teen, that's one of the things I always associated with the pirate stations – the smell of drink and tobacco. Almost every pirate radio station operated from a studio that was a dive and, looking back on it, the equipment was a total joke. But, despite it all, it was like a drug to a lot of us. Pirate radio had a magic that I've never seen before or since.

'I started with CCLR around 1981 and I went on to other pirate stations. Radio Caroline broadcast from a mobile home in Togher and there was quite a few of us working there – myself, PJ Coogan, Ken Tobin, Trevor Welch, Rob Allen and Colin Edwards. The guys around in radio at my time generally worked together. You'd all work for one station and, when that closed down, you'd move on to the station that would open up in its place.

'It was all cloak-and-dagger stuff. There were budgets for absolutely nothing. If I wanted to give away a prize on the radio I had to go down to a shop myself and ask whether they would sponsor a CD or a voucher. For the most part, people would sponsor products – a furniture store might sponsor a chair as a prize or a department store might sponsor some perfume. That's the way it was.

'I remember the first prize I ever gave away on air was for a grandfather-style shirt. The winner lived on Pearse Road in Ballyphehane and I dropped the prize out to her directly as I was driving home with my Dad. I can't drive past that house today without thinking of CCLR and my first on-air prize.

'Later it was the same thing on SouthCoast. If you wanted an echo chamber to work on a jingle or a voice-over, you used an old piece of Wavin pipe or a toilet-role insert. We would sometimes work up jingles by going down to Patrick Street and asking schoolgirls on their lunch break to sing "SouthCoast" into the microphone and then get them to chant the names of the various DJs onto the tape. It was that sophisticated.

'As for the characters, it was a hilarious time to be in radio. The old story goes: "You don't have to be mad to work in this industry but it certainly helps." It's a very unique thing to sit in a studio for up to four hours and talk to people you don't know. In a certain way, you can't be sane. The characters at that time were incredible.

'There was a father and son. Roger Ryan, who was a country and western buff, was on CCLR. He would finish his programme on a Tuesday night at 9 p.m. and his son, who was also called Roger Ryan, would come on air with the "handle" Paul Young. He had a rock show. I think there was one night when Roger finished with Johnny Cash's "Ring of Fire" and his son took over and started his show with AC/DC and "Whole Lotta Rosie".

'It was an era when almost anything went. It was a bit of a free-for-all. There was no such thing as programming controls, playlists or anything like that. But I think that is what made it so special. It was a magic time. You turned on the radio and you never quite knew what was coming up next.

'I actually started out on radio as Paul Byrne in CCLR but then I became Paul Stevens. Later on I went to the old SouthCoast and, because they had a guy called Don Stevens, I had to change my name to Paul Davis. And that seemed to work fine.

'Like most of the other lads, I started playing discos. If pirate radio was our FÁS training ground, discos were the real deal in that they paid your bills. They were also a great way of getting feedback about your show and what people thought of your broadcasting.

'I started playing De Lacy House and you'd finish at 2 a.m. and, for some strange reason, we were drawn back over to the radio station. Someone would be on air and you would go in and chat to them or maybe broadcast yourself. There was something special about the stations back then – you just loved being around them.

'Anyone who knows me will testify that there is nothing I love more than a bit of craic. I love a bit of humour, having a laugh and joke with friends and colleagues. For me, it is such an important part of life. Even to this day, I'm an awful man for pranks. I remember in SouthCoast, Pearse McCarthy, who is now a news reader in 96FM, was going to Presentation Brothers College (PBC) and he would come in after school and hang around the station dreaming of being on air.

'We all took an instant liking to him because he is a lovely guy. One time, he came in with a Pres scarf and we cut it up into strips to add to the Christmas decorations around the studio. His mother rang later looking for him at the studio and someone told her Pearse was gone down to the pub drinking with the lads, which needless to say he hadn't because he was only fifteen. I think she slaughtered him when he got home.

'I remember another time when Rob Allen was about to read the news in SouthCoast, when they were based on North Main Street. I was hanging around the studio and I spotted a newspaper lying nearby and I couldn't resist it – I put a match to it and put it underneath Rob as he was trying to read the news. In fairness to Rob, his seat was smoking and his ass was probably scorched but he kept reading the news without a break.

'Fergal Barry, who was another newsreader for SouthCoast, was another schoolboy. He would come into the studio at 7 a.m. every day to read the news at 8.45 a.m. before going up to school. His news would be recorded and we'd play the same bulletin right up to lunchtime when it would be changed. But one day the tape snarled right in the middle of Fergal's bulletin, so he got a slagging from his mates in school and we had to change the whole news pre-recording system.

'It was hilarious at times in some pirate stations. There was a lovely guy working in ERI called John O'Connor. John was actually a workaholic. He never took a holiday and worked really, really hard. John was like a lot of us in pirate radio in that we were afraid to take time off. You felt that if you took a holiday or a bit of time away, your slot would be gone when you got back.

'John was on air one day and, of course, was doing the work of two or three people. He was an incredible operator who was hugely talented. But he got flustered coming up to the bulletin and, when introducing the news, went: "Good day, it's Three O'Connor, I'm John O'Clock." Ever since that moment his nickname was "The Clocker". There were so many stories like that.

'There was another really hard-working guy there called Jim Reid. He never slept – he always seemed to be around the station. A few of us joked that we thought he was actually living in the studio because he was always there. Late one night I was listening to his show and as the record came to an end all of a sudden there was total silence. I thought the transmitter had gone down until I started to hear the sound of snoring. Poor Jim was so exhausted, he fell asleep live on air. He was snoring and grunting live on air – when he would stop snoring for a few seconds you could actually hear the studio clock ticking in the background.

'There was another very small pirate radio station, I think it was called Centre Radio, based over by the North Mall. I rang them up one night pretending to be someone else and, to tell you how primitive it was, the DJ was physically holding the receiver of the telephone up to the microphone to broadcast audience comments. We were just taking the piss out of them because they were our rivals. I think I came out with a few mad comments before they cut me off.

'There was another DJ called Tom Cunneen who called himself DJ Thoma. He used to play oldies on a Sunday morning on CCLR. Tom was the most unorganised person you could ever come across. We used to use cassettes for the ads or jingles. Tom was playing something like Bobby Darin from 1967 and it was the height of summer. He introduced a break on the show and then played an advert for Christmas. But Tom, quick as a flash, came back on air and saved the day with: "On this show, even the ads are old." It was classic.

'The characters were unbelievable at the time. Who could ever forget Romano Macari? Everyone in Cork knew him – he was a household name. It was brilliant talk radio and while at times the programme was a bit all over the place, that is what made it interesting. You never quite knew what was going to come up on the programme and that is why people tuned in.

'SouthCoast was incredible at the time. They were amongst the first of the so-called super pirate stations. But it was a wonderful station and I don't think there has ever been a station like it since. It seemed to have a buzz about it – you tuned in and, before you knew it, you'd be smiling. They had a sound that I have never heard anyone rival. You only have to look at the people working there who went on to have major national careers.

'You had people like Henry Condon and Pete O'Neill – they showed that Cork radio guys were every bit as good as the British lads that dominated pirate radio at the start. To be honest, Henry and Pete are amongst the best radio guys Ireland has ever seen. They had two of the finest broadcast voices I've ever heard. But they weren't really interested in being in front of the microphone – they loved radio in a totally different way to say someone like me.

'ERI was a very serious station. There was a lot of money put into their equipment and operations. They also poached people from other stations. But I don't think their sound was ever as good as SouthCoast. They had a very good set-up, good DJs and really excellent broadcasting gear. But their greatest asset was John Creedon who is one of my all-time heroes in radio broadcasting. John has it all: a great voice, lovely presenting style and the common touch which makes him such a wonderful people's person. When John is on air you always get the feeling that he is talking directly to you.

'I loved radio but, if I'm honest, it was actually broadcasting I was in love with. And, having shown I could do radio, I began to fancy trying my hand at TV. As the years went by, I wanted to get involved in TV. It began for me when I was doing stage shows and discos around Cork and I started to introduce items based on the great British chat and game shows. Items like "Blankety Blank", "Blind Date" and "Play the Game". I loved it and that is what got me interested in TV.

'It was Ken Tobin who told me that Cork Multichannel was looking to recruit people. I hadn't heard about it and, at the time, I didn't have multichannel TV. I had an accident and was in hospital – don't laugh but I was electrocuted doing a disco down in Ardmore in County Waterford. I had applied to Cork Multichannel and got a call to say I had an audition on Monday at 3 p.m. on George's Quay. I had to discharge myself from hospital to go and do the audition. But I was so ill I almost collapsed on George's Quay afterwards.

'I spent five days at home in bed before I was able to go back to the studio. I got the gig in Cork Multichannel and it was my big break, looking on it now. I did a lot of stuff with them – it was a great training ground. My aim was to do light entertainment – I loved the whole game show industry.

'I was fifteen when I started in pirate radio and it was the beginning of ten years of constant fun for me. I got into the height of trouble for some of the fun and pranks I got involved in. It was all innocent fun but I suppose the times were changing in Ireland, the money was beginning to flow into radio and TV stations and people were getting very serious and very professional and they just took a dim view to that type of innocent fun. No one was hurt or defamed, it was mostly winding people up, but that time had passed.'

'I always remember the night the old SouthCoast shut down up in St Luke's. It was Friday, July 13th. Mick O'Brien had called us all up to say there was a meeting. Keith York, God rest him, was the DJ and he was playing non-stop music that had a theme of goodbye. I knew we were in trouble. His last record was Abba's 'Thank You For The Music'. It was one of the saddest days I've known. It was like losing a member of your family – it might sound strange but that's how we felt because the station was, in a way, like our work family.

'There was a big van outside and we were all asked to help move the studio gear out into it. We all chipped in but Don Stevens refused to help because he said: 'I came here to build a radio station not to close one down.' We all just thought he was a lazy bastard who didn't want to help us. It was such a sad day for Cork.

'When Radio South got the licence in 1989, I was involved in its early days. I used to do a show from 10 p.m. until 2 a.m. called *Into The Night*. I hated it. I came from Cork Multichannel to do it and I knew from the very beginning that it just wasn't me. My heart had moved on from radio. I was on better money than I was in Cork Multichannel but I was bored with the slot. I think I lasted a year before I called a halt to it.'

'I joined TV3 when it started up in 1998 and I haven't looked back since. I'm based in Cork, I get to set my own news agenda and I generally cover all of Munster for TV3. I've also been able to work on special documentaries which have been a great thrill. I work a general news beat but I still love light entertainment. When I listen to radio now it is mostly to catch the news headlines. But I still tune in to Neil Prendeville and PJ Coogan on RedFM and 96FM when I can.

'I once heard a guy describe stations like RedFM, 96FM, 98FM and FM104 as "Hoover radio". They are literally sucking in listeners by cash give-aways, prize draws, competitions and the like. Radio is big business now and nothing stands in the way of building audience share and keeping the ad men and the directors happy. It is an era of playlists, radio doctors and the like. I can understand why but it is not for me. I think I worked in radio at the best possible time and, if I went back, I think I'd be sad at what I'd find.'

CHAPTER ELEVEN

Noel Welch, aka Noel Evans: 'Pirate radio is now a distant memory for many of us, but it struck a blow for pioneering DJs everywhere when stations first hit the airwaves in Cork in the late 1970s. It was fresh, very risky and a bit of a novelty. We hadn't heard anything like it before. The pirates of the airwaves set the tone for pop radio in this country.

'As for the Cork Broadcasting Company (CBC), CCLR, Radio City, and SouthCoast, all of which I had the pleasure of spinning my discs on, they all remain part of a happy time, long gone, but forever etched in the memories of its many listeners.

'My first introduction to pirate radio in Cork was listening to the band Blondie singing "Denis" on CBC. The station came on the scene out of nowhere and I was thrilled to hear that they were looking for DJs. This would have been in February 1978. They had placed an advertisement in *The Evening Echo* which I had spotted. I was working as an apprentice compositor in *The Echo* and the advert literally jumped off the page at me.

'I was always interested in radio. I was doing DJ gigs in my late teens, and I loved it. I was an avid radio fan and, to be honest, when I saw the advert I didn't think "oh, pirate radio" I just thought "radio, this is my chance". I loved the idea of combining my love of music and my growing music collection with something like a radio show.

'It was a bit daunting at first, as there was absolutely no radio or broadcasting background in my family. I had no problem working as a DJ in clubs and the like but radio was the glamorous, exciting world that we knew very little about. Just being asked for a demo tape was daunting because I had little recording equipment of my own to make a proper demo.

'So, I borrowed my uncle Tony's bright red radio-cassette player and went out to his house in Muskerry Estate in Ballincollig, sat down in his kitchen and wrote out a script. I brought out a few vinyl singles and introduced those. It was all spur-of-the-moment stuff and I thought I hadn't a hope of getting a radio slot with a demo like that. But it was the best I could do in the circumstances and I wanted to give CBC every shot.

'I also had to keep the whole thing quiet because I had a full-time job with *The Echo* and I didn't know how they would react to me getting involved with a radio station. At the time, newspapers were seen as serious media and any radio station that wasn't RTÉ was kind of regarded with some suspicion. I suppose, looking back on it, I regarded radio as a bit of a hobby. I wasn't involved in sport so I had a bit of time on my hands and I saw it as the perfect way of combining something with my love of music.

'I popped the demo cassette into an envelope, posted it and waited to see what would happen next. I always remember I had to send it to a DJ Daniels who ran a disco equipment shop on MacCurtain Street. I think the address for CBC at the time was Wilton Gardens.

'About three days later I received a letter in the post. I opened it really slowly because I thought I hadn't a hope of getting a gig with them and was preparing myself for rejection.

Stevie Bolger, aka DJ Chris Stevens, striking a pose

Pat Egan with Phil Lynott and
Rory Gallagher

An advert for a disc jockey for
Eastside Radio Ireland (ERI)

Dan Noonan, aka DJ Karl Johnson, in the studios of
Radio City in the early 1980s

John Creedon, centre, with leather jacket, with other radio DJs

Left
John Craig, Mark Bell, Tony Allen, Geoff Harris and Pat O'Rourke

Below
The late Dominic O'Keeffe, aka DJ Domino, left, with Noel Welch

A young Henry Condon with John Kenny on SouthCoast Radio.
John later went on to work on RTÉ Sport

Nick Richards choosing a disc for his pirate radio show

The late Keith Yorke on SouthCoast Radio

The late Hugh Browne on SouthCoast Radio

The studios of CBC on Penrose Wharf, where the station was broadcasting from in the early 1980s

The basement studios of Cork Broadcasting Company (CBC), in the late 1970s, on Patrick's Hill

A recent get-together of pirate radio DJs. Back row: Tony Whitnell, aka DJ Top Cat; Noel Welch, aka DJ Noel Evans; Paul Byrne, aka DJ Paul Davis. Front row: Trevor Welch, aka DJ Trevor Stevens; Dan Noonan, aka DJ Karl Johnson; Ken Tobin, aka DJ Steve Davis

TP/KLW

A letter to Noel Welch from Tony
Prince of Radio Luxembourg

2nd May, 1978

Noel Welch,
4 Edward Walsh Road,
Togher Cork City,
Ireland

Dear Noel

Many thanks for your inquiry into our Celebrity D.J. spot.

If you would be kind enough to send me an audition tape or
cassette of approximately ten minutes duration, I will
give it a good listen and write back to say whether
we could offer you a spot on Celebrity D.J.'s.

Look forward to hearing from you in the near future.

Yours sincerely

TONY PRINCE
Programme Director

IT'S THE
STARLIGHT
RADIO SHOW

Tune In

APRIL 6TH 78

NOW IT'S THE TURN OF
THE CORK PIRATES TO
CHALLENGE R.T.E.

● JACK LYNCH TAKES THE SALUTE AS THE C.B.S. CAR PASSES IN THE ST. PATRICKS DAY PARADE.

Opening Day
Thursday 31 May 1979

Up to the minute News every hour
on the half-hour and at midnight,
1.00 a.m. and Closedown, with
major sports results as they come
to hand.

12.30 RTE RADIO 2, ON THE AIR
pm   The Minister for Posts &
Telegraphs, Mr. Padraig Faulkner
inaugurates RTE's second National
Radio Service. Introduced from
Studio 1 by Brendan Balfe.

12.35 POP AROUND IRELAND
pm   Musical greetings across the
country to celebrate the opening of
RTE Radio 2
with Larry Gogan in Dublin
Vincent Hanley in Drogheda
Ronan Collins in Athlone
Marty Whelan in Limerick
Áine Hensey in Galway
Mark Cagney in Cork
Paschal Mooney in Sligo
Geoff Harris in Waterford
and
Candy Devine, Downtown
Radio, Belfast.

Co-ordinating Producers:
Louis Hogan and Cathal MacCabe

5.00 WHEELIN' HOME — From Limerick
pm   Whether you're on the road or
waiting at home, Marty Whelan
brings you the best in music, traffic
information, Call in the Country
and the Five Day Quiz.

Producer: Robbie Irwin

7.00 THE HEATHER BREEZE — From
pm   Galway
The world of traditional and folk
music with Áine Hensey. Clár da
theangacht le cheol traidisiúnta is
nua-aoiseach.

Producer: Fiach O Broin

8.00 KEEP IT COUNTRY — From Sligo
pm   **Paschal Mooney's** twice weekly
country show.

Producer: Bili O'Donovan

10.00 NIGHT MOVES — From Cork
pm   With **Mark Cagney**
Including a two-way link up with
Glenn Richards in BBC Radio
Ulster.
Ring 021-25248 for your Pop
Requests.

Producer: Aidan Stanley

12.00 DAVE FANNING ROCKS
am   The Definitive Rock Show

Producer: Ian Wilson

2.00 CLOSEDOWN
am

FOR THE LAST two months
the airwaves of Cork have been
enjoying an injection of fresh
sounds, new voices, and up to
the minute local information.
All this is packaged and presented on 230 metres, on the
medium wave band, and is
called Cork Broadcasting
Company.
The Station comes on the air
each morning at 8.00 a.m. and
goes out live right through the
day to 8.00 p.m. From 8.00
a.m. to 11.00 a.m. Dave Porter
presents his "Good Morning
Cork" programme; from 11.00
a.m. to 2.00 p.m. it's "Sounds
Like Chris Stevens"; from 2.00
p.m. to 5.00 p.m. it's "Afternoon Delights" with Noel
Evans and from 5.00 p.m. to
8.00 p.m. it's the "King Tony
Show".
Through the day there are up

to the minute traffic reports, as
Cork has probably the worse
traffic problems anywhere in
Ireland (the local Co-op Taxi
Company keep them in-
formed). All items of local
interest are dealt with
throughout the day with roving
reporter John Dolan covering
the stories as they happen.
The success the station is
enjoying has amazed everyone,
including the directors who are:
D.J. Daniels — well known for
his Sound and Lighting Shop;
Steve Bolger — well known in
entertainment circles and Co-
Director of Swingers Night
Club and Con McParland who
lectures in Electronics.
On Friday, March 17th,
C.B.S. made a little history by
entering the St. Patrick's Day
parade in Cork City and
upstaged a lot of the bigger

exhibits on the day. Using three
sports cars, simply covered in
C.B.C. car stickers and playing
good music that was being
transmitted from their studios,
the station was cheered and
back slapped from beginning to
end of the parade. They claim
Jack Lynch even gave them a
little wave as they passed the
reviewing stand. En route the
station personnel distributed no
less than ten thousand leaflets
giving information on times of
broadcasting etc.
The Station was raided on
Wednesday last, however, and
had much of its equipment
confiscated. D.J. Daniels and
Stevie Bolger were in court the
following day to challenge the
seizure. They lost the first
round, however, but say the
battle will continue. Meanwhile
C.B.C. is back on the air.

**RLIGHT Top 20 on
Radio Dublin every Sat...1-2 p.m.**

Newspaper clippings of various trials and tribulations

"Pirate" group's court bid fails

An injunction seeking to prevent further raids on a pirate radio station in Cork and the return of equipment confiscated last Wednesday afternoon was refused in the High Court in Dublin yesterday.

Mr. Justice Hamilton said he would not make an order to inhibit what was in effect the law of this country. It was quite clear that the authorities were entitled to confiscate equipment under the provisions of the Wireless Telegraph Act 1926 and he would express no opinion on whether or not the Act was constitutional.

The plaintiffs in the action were Daniel Walsh, Stephen Bolger and Con McPartland with an address at 7 Farley Place, Montenotte, Cork. In an affidavit they were described as radio broadcasters who had been operating a station playing mostly pop music since last January.

During that time their advertising revenue had amounted to almost £2,000. Last Wednesday afternoon detectives, gardai and officials from the Department of Posts and Telegraphs raided their premises in Montenotte and confiscated equipment, including their transmitter, worth £3,000.

Outlining the plaintiffs case Mr. James O'Driscoll S.C. said the claim was for an injunction to stop the authorities from repeating what they had done the previous day. Equipment had been confiscated under Section 8 of the Wireless Telegraph Act 1926 and under that section there did not appear to be any remedy to have the equipment returned.

He challenged that Act on the grounds that it was in direct contradiction to Article 46 (1) of the Constitution. Mr. O'Driscoll submitted that the Court should come to the aid of the plaintiffs pending determination of the Constitutionality of the Act. The Constitution envisaged the operation of radio stations such as his clients were operating subject to public order and morality. Mere broadcasting per se was not in contravention of public order and morality.

Mr. Justice Hamilton: Your are asking me fo permit your clients to continue to break the law. Your clients have been in breach of the law. He said he would have to accept the law as Constitutional until it was found to be otherwise.

Mr. James O'Driscoll S.C. and Mr. Nicholas Kearns B.L., instructed by Mr. Rory Conway, solicitor, were for the plaintiffs. There was no appearance for the defence.

Cork protest at golf tournament

To officially launch International Anti-Apartheid Year as declared by the United Nations, a crowd of over 100 people attended a slide show and lecture at Connolly Hall, jointly sponsored by the Cork Anti-Apartheid Movement and the ICTU. Keith Haight, formerly a lecturer in Southern African history at the University of San Francisco, gave a brief history of the development of apartheid in South Africa, entitled "Soweto — Key to South Africa's future?"

The slides, with commentary read by Eamonn Noonan and Frank Ryan, covered the history of the Soweto riots and sympathetic uprisings all round the country.

Charles Hayes, of the East Cork AAM, discussed the role of boycotts in the fight against apartheid. If we were to chose persuasion rather than bloodshed, he argued, boycotts were the only course. He stressed that the "keep politics out of sport"

Raid on 'pirate' station

GARDAI and officials of the Department of Posts and Telegraphs carried out a raid on Cork's commercial radio station "Cork Broadcasting Company" yesterday afternoon and seized £3,000 worth of equipment, including the company's transmitter.

The station has been broadcasting on 230 metres medium waveband from a private house in the Montenotte area of the city for two months.

The raid was carried out by five uniformed gardai, two Dublin detectives and three officials of the Department.

Chris Stevens, disc jockey, said: "I was in the middle of broadcasting my mid-morning show and had just introduced Don McClean's 'Living With The Blues' when I heard a knock on the studio door. Thinking it was Dave Porter I opened the door to find the men in blue on the threshold and with a search warrant in their hands.

"No resistance was offered and after the officials had informed me of their intentions I advised our listeners that we were going off the air," said Mr. Stevens.

The operators of the station are to seek an injunction against the Minister for Posts and Telegraphs in the High Court in Dublin today to prevent a similar raid being carried out and they are also seeking the return of the seized equipment.

Raids sink Pirates

CORK'S three unlicensed radio stations, Alternative Broadcasting, Cork; Cork Broadcasting Company and Cork City Radio, went off the air yesterday.

It followed raids on the premises of the first two by members of the Department of Posts and Telegraphs accompanied by members of the gardai, while Cork City Radio were reported to have ceased transmitting following a tip-off.

The total value of the equipment confiscated in A.B.C. and C.B.C. is understood to be valued in all at around £6,000.

A statement from A.B.C. said they were visited at 12.05 p.m. and a programme being presented by their disc jockey was interrupted.

"The station," said the statement, "was then closed down and equipment, including a transmitter, deck units, jingle machine and accessories were confiscated by the members of P.&T.

"As no resistance or delay was experienced none of the equipment was damaged and P.&T. officials stated to our disc jockey that all the equipment would be returned in time with the exception of the transmitter, valued at £1,500."

Their station is in the Montenotte area and the C.B.C. station is in the Patrick's Hill area, while the C.C.R. station is in the flat of the city.

An A.B.C. spokesman said last night they would be working throughout the night to get back on the air.

Then, lo and behold, they were offering me a position on the station. There was no interview, just a note to say that I could start immediately if I was available.

'This was around March 1978 and it was coming up to St Patrick's Day. I met the lads at CBC prior to the Bank Holiday weekend and it was a little bit cloak-and-dagger. The studio was in a block of flats opposite The Country Club (now The Montenotte Hotel) and I had to knock and wait to be escorted up. The guy I met that day was Stevie Bolger who was well known within the nightclub scene in Cork. I'd heard a lot about Stevie but I had never met him before that day. He was a Dub who had come down to Cork and was running Good Time Charlies. He had a lot of experience of DJs so I felt comfortable straight away.

'I brought about six or seven records with me and he asked me was I ready to go on air straightaway. The equipment was basic enough so all you needed was a five-minute crash course in what to do. If you were used to working as a DJ in a nightclub you pretty much knew what was involved. I was told I was going on right after Stevie. He asked me what my name was and I looked at him as if he had two heads. I said: "I'm Noel Welch." He shook his head and told me that I couldn't go on air using my own name – I had to come up with an alias. Stevie told me to think about it for a minute and he'd be back to me.

'I had been listening to BBC Radio 1 and I was a fan of Noel Edmunds, who of course went on to become a big TV star in the UK in the 1980s and 1990s. I loved his style of presenting so I thought I'd stick with Noel. I considered my surname, "Welch", and wondered what a typical Welsh surname was? "Evans" popped into my head and that was it – I was going on air as Noel Evans. Of course, Stevie then introduced me as Dale Evans. I still have no idea where that came from. But I stuck with Noel Evans and that was my handle throughout my time in pirate radio.

'Around that time I was working as a DJ with a Cork band called Jigsaw. I grew up with the lads and I was helping them out as a support DJ. Back then, the DJ would go on before the band, whereas now, it is the DJ who wraps up the night. My first DJ gig with them was down in the Cobh Community Hall and I will never forget arriving with only four records. I managed to squeeze a one-hour performance from those four records that night. I think those kind of experiences helped when it came to radio.

'I remember going to England on holidays in the late 1970s and BBC Radio 1 were broadcasting live from the motor racing circuit at Brands Hatch. My uncle, Don, brought me up there and I got to meet most of the Radio 1 presenters who, to me, were like rock stars at the time. I remember going up to Noel Edmunds and saying "Hi, my name is Noel Evans", almost as if he would take it as a tribute. Looking back, I was as excited getting to meet those jocks as a lifelong Manchester United fan getting to meet the entire first team on the morning of an FA Cup final.

'Later on I got to meet the BBC's David Hamilton who was another guy I had a lot of respect for. Tony Prince on Radio Luxembourg was also a hero of mine and I got to meet him face-to-face many years later. David Hamilton came over to Good Time Charlies and I was sent over by *The Echo* to do an interview with him. When the interview was over, I asked him about work for the BBC and he stared at me in amazement. I will always remember the advice he gave me, which was to start local and work my way up the broadcasting ladder.

'Tony Prince said much the same thing when I met him at Krojacks nightclub in Carey's Lane, off Patrick Street. It was one of the top clubs in the city and they brought Tony over for a special weekend gig as guest DJ. He was a lovely guy and, when I asked about working for Radio Luxembourg, he told me to put a demo tape together and send it directly to him. I took him up on his offer and, to this day, I still have his reply on the Radio Luxembourg headed notepaper. He listened to it but said it wasn't quite what they were looking for – in fairness to the man he let me down easy. It certainly wasn't up to the standard that they were used to out in the Grand Duchy.

'It was hilarious at the time. The lads in work, when they realised I had a gig on CBC, started calling me "Noel Evans" rather than my real name. I'd get slagged about the music or playing specific requests for people. It is amazing the impact the station had in the short time it was around. Once people realised you were on radio, it transformed the way you were treated at gigs.

'There was a kind of rock star glamour about the whole DJ and pirate radio world. At the time, I drove an old white Ford Capri with a black vinyl roof. My record box was holding up the back seat because the hinge was broken. I parked opposite the studio and I never really had any great fears of the station being raided. The lads behind CBC always said that if the Gardaí or inspectors from the Department of Posts and Telegraphs ever arrived they were to be allowed in immediately. We were to co-operate with them.

'Within a couple of weeks, the CBC operation was getting really professional. They had special jingles organised and every DJ got their own for their show. I was delighted. The equipment started to get better and everyone who was involved wanted to improve their radio skills – none of us were in it for

131

the money. I think every single one of us saw pirate radio as a stepping stone to a career in broadcasting.

'It is amazing, looking back on it now, just how many of the lads that got their start with CBC went on to become national broadcasters. There were a lot of award-winning broadcasters who came through that station in the short time it was around. None of us realised it, but CBC and other pirate radio stations were like a training academy for RTÉ's 2FM and the commercial radio stations that would eventually come on the scene.

'It was all about the music. Young people just weren't getting their favourite music played on RTÉ Radio 1 and they were desperate to hear the bands they liked. That is why so many people who grew up in the 1970s loved the BBC and Radio Luxembourg. RTÉ eventually got their act together with 2FM from 1979 but before then it is easy to understand why the pirate radio stations made such an impact.

'DJs tended to move around. As pirate stations would close or transform into other stations. You had rival stations setting up and the entire industry started to get more professional and better resourced. DJs might have a good gig with one station but then get the offer of a better slot with another one. Some stations would close after a garda raid and then re-emerge under another name.

'CBC was a great start for me. The station eventually moved from the flat in St Luke's to St Patrick's Hill. It operated from a basement and it was a one-man operation. If you were on duty you did everything – checked the post, presented the show, made the tea and answered calls to the door.

'I was there one day and, when you were on air, you were at eye level with the roadway outside. I had been running late that day and had parked directly outside on a double-yellow line. Out of the corner of my eye, I spotted the traffic warden in the distance. I had to grab a long-playing record, put that on, lock up the studio, run out to move my car and drive it to a "no disc" parking zone. I then legged it back down to the studio before the record finished, praying all the while that the record hadn't skipped.

'CBC was a shoestring operation but we didn't see it like that. We wanted to be every bit as professional as the lads in RTÉ. I think it is also interesting to remember that Cork people regarded us in a totally different light to what you might read in the newspapers or in government press releases about "pirate radio". We had a huge fan base and had incredible access across the entertainment industry because of that.

'Any big act that came to play in Cork invariably ended up giving interviews to CBC, Radio City and later SouthCoast and ERI. I remember having Paul Brady on my show with CBC just a couple of hours before he went on stage at the City Hall. Thin Lizzy, U2, The Boomtown Rats and Aslan all appeared on Cork pirate radio stations in the late 1970s and early 1980s. They wanted to plug their albums and their gigs and were only too happy to do that on local radio. But you had to do your research. If you didn't, the word went out pretty quickly and the next big acts in Cork wouldn't do your show; they would appear on someone else's. So you made sure you knew everything about the band, their music, their tour plans and their history.

'After St Patrick's Hill, CBC moved to Penrose Quay to a second-floor studio. They were the best studios we'd had. There was plenty of studio space and we had large windows looking out over the city and the quays. But that was my last studio with CBC, as I moved the short distance to Radio City, on Parnell Place, a short time later. With CBC I had been presenting a show called *Afternoon Delights*. I think this would have been around 1979 or 1980. The station was run by Dan Noonan, aka DJ Karl Johnson, and I knew him from my work as a nightclub DJ. He had presented on CBC and then decided to break away and set up his own station. There was some new talent brought in and one of those was Susan James, who was, in real life, Susan O'Connor, from the O'Connor funeral directors family. I worked with Susan on a hospitals request show. We put request boxes in hospitals around Cork and did a Saturday morning show especially for people in the North Infirmary, Mercy, South Infirmary, St Finbarr's, or Cork Regional Hospital, as it was then.

'I was very lucky at the time in that I had a full-time job and a decent income. So I was comfortable and didn't have to worry about making a living from working as a DJ or radio "jock". I was about five years with *The Evening Echo* at that stage. I joined them in 1973 straight out of school and eventually worked for them for over forty years, retiring in 2014. I never saw radio as a financial gig. I went to radio because I loved music and it gave me a chance to combine broadcasting with my greatest hobby and some of my favourite bands.

'Most of my spare time was spent going to see bands play in City Hall or The Stardust. Radio was just an extension of that. Music was hugely important to people at the time – you had the tail end of the showband era with a hugely exciting folk and rock scene. If you couldn't make it to live shows, radio was your only option because RTÉ, before 2FM, largely ignored that scene, with the exception of Larry Gogan and his Top 40 show.

'I know a lot of people say the 1960s was the golden era for music but I think the 1970s and 1980s get overlooked. In the

1970s you had the whole rock scene, then you had disco and finally you had the punk revolution. People were really passionate about the music they liked and even having a cassette player in your car was a big deal back then. Almost everyone had a radio in their car and that is what made pirate radio stations so special – they gave you the keys to a world that no one else could.

'Disco eventually killed off the showband scene which had been slowly dying for about ten years. It is hard to explain to people today the kind of impact that The BeeGees and *Saturday Night Fever* had on the social scene. Discos became the only option and the old showband halls began to switch over to the nightclub scene.

'It was a godsend for DJs because every club wanted the best "jocks" and were willing to pay for the privilege. Of course, if you were presenting your own show on pirate radio, you were pretty much at the top of the queue to be hired for the best clubs. That is where the money was – in the nightclubs rather than the radio stations. In a way, one funded the other. In an era before *Hot Press*, the so-called bible of the Irish music scene was the magazine *Spotlight*, and they had a big photo feature on CBC. That's the level of "street cred" that the pirate radio stations had back then.

'CBC was ahead of its time given the way it was professionally run and tapped into what was happening on the Cork social and music scene. Stevie and Don (Walsh) really delivered a winner and it is just a pity that the station didn't stick around longer.

'I don't think you can overstate the impact pirate radio stations had on people's lives. Remember this was an era before mobile phones, before the Internet and social media and before multichannel TV. We were getting requests by the bucketload on CBC and then Radio City – and imagine the time it took for a person to write a letter or a postcard, go to the post office, pay for a stamp and then mail it. But tens of thousands of people did that because they wanted their music played. I will never forget the sense of astonishment at the level of response we'd get to some shows.

'What made it special was that you got to know your audience and your listeners. Some people would call by the studio to hand-deliver a request or a letter. They'd be thrilled with the music or the fact that you mentioned their item on air. It was a level of contact with the public that none of us ever imagined possible.

'For a time I did think about going into radio full-time. I'd asked about jobs in both the BBC and Radio Luxembourg and didn't get anywhere. Then, in 1979, 2FM was rolled out by RTÉ and they were looking for anchor presenters from Cork, Limerick and Galway. I simply had to apply for it and I was called for an interview over in Union Quay, where RTÉ had their Cork offices back then.

'The guy that got the job was Stevie Bolger. He got in with 2FM just as they were taking off which was a fantastic break for him. I didn't make it and, if I'm honest, I can understand why Stevie got the nod – he is an excellent radio presenter. The job came up maybe two or three years too early for me. I just didn't have the radio experience that Stevie had at that point. But I went up to Dublin for the launch of 2FM because a friend of mine from Waterford, Geoff Harris, who had also worked in CBC, got a slot with RTÉ and he invited me up for it. I remember we were all in the pub after the official launch and I found myself sitting beside Gerry Ryan.

'He was so young and I will never forget turning to him and asking what it was like working for RTÉ? He was such a nice fella and he replied: "It's great but I could be gone tomorrow. You just don't know." I said to him: "Gerry, you won't be gone tomorrow. You have your leg inside the door and just keep doing what got you here." Who knew that he would go on to become such a legend in Irish broadcasting? But that was the problem with RTÉ – it was so, so hard to get your foot in the door in the first place.

'But there were so many talented DJs on the scene at that time, most of whom worked in Cork either through pirate radio or the local clubs. Vincent Hanley, of course, worked in Cork nightclubs before he got his break with RTÉ. Then you also had Mark Cagney and John Creedon. The good thing was that when these guys got their break with RTÉ and headed to Dublin, it opened up possibilities for the rest of us in Cork. For instance, Mark Cagney replaced Vincent Hanley in Good Time Charlies and, when Mark moved on, I got his job. I thought it was my stepping stone to RTÉ but it didn't quite work out that way. I think I always considered *The Echo* as my full-time, bread-and-butter job and maybe that was a factor in the whole thing.

'In fact, I probably had it better than almost any of the other lads because I had a full-time income from the newspaper, I had my radio gig with CBC and then Radio City, plus I had the work with the various nightclubs and that was becoming very well paid. So part of the scenario for me was that I had the best of both worlds.

'I went as far as I could with pirate radio and I enjoyed every minute of it. After CBC and Radio City I worked with CCLR and SouthCoast. But one of the things I'm proudest of was the role I played with Cork Hospital Radio. Hospital radio was huge in the UK and Europe and it slowly dawned on me that there wasn't much of it here, particularly not in Cork. There was some hospital radio in the Mater in Dublin. So I decided, along with Tadhg Dolan, another great CBC DJ, to set up Cork Hospital Radio back in 1988.

'Cork Regional Hospital, which of course is now Cork University Hospital, gave us the green light very quickly and we went on air reasonably quickly. It is a very different operation to pirate radio or even commercial radio but it is hugely rewarding in terms of the difference you can make to people at a critical time in their lives. I'm really proud of the fact that, twenty-seven years later, Cork Hospital Radio is still going strong today. There are only a handful of stations around Ireland – I certainly wish there were more – but the work they do is absolutely incredible.

'It is very much in the spirit of pirate radio – it is all about dedication and volunteerism. There isn't any money involved and people generally stay involved for the love of the work. That is what happened with pirate radio in the 1970s and 1980s. It was a bunch of people who absolutely loved music and presenting radio programmes. That came across in everything they did and I think that is why people have such fond memories of the Cork pirates to this day.'

CHAPTER TWELVE
The Craic

Part of the nostalgia that now surrounds Cork's pirate radio stations concerns the sheer sense of fun that pervaded them.

Without exception, every single DJ that contributed to this book admitted they had never before, or since, experienced the sheer joy of working in the Cork pirate stations of the late 1970s and early 1980s. Most never realised it at the time but they were experiencing the happiest work years of their careers. Most would never again experience the sheer sense of fun and excitement that each station seemed to effortlessly generate.

It is important to remember that the early pirate stations weren't set up with an overwhelmingly commercial focus – they were almost like clubs set up by friends to play the music that wasn't being played elsewhere. Music rather than money was the rule. It's not that money wasn't important at the time – it always is – just that it wasn't the almighty determining factor that it became with the later commercial stations.

That sense of fun was influenced as much by the atmosphere in the stations as it was by the personnel. 'Things happened then that would never happen today – or if they did they would give a station manager a heart attack,' Noel Welch recalled. 'But it was a different era. Can you imagine RTÉ or Today FM or Newstalk taking a teenager off the street, listening to their demo tape and agreeing to put them live on air that very same night? Not a chance. But that is what happened with the pirate stations in Cork.'

In almost all cases, the pirate stations were making up their rules as they went along, in many cases through a process of trial and error. Playlists, audience share and market demographics were things no one had ever heard of. Many DJs worked for free or at least for a pittance. Most brought their own records to the station and, in almost all cases, the studio wasn't just a workplace, it doubled as a sort of social clubhouse.

The combination of a lax, if almost non-existent, rule book, combined with an overwhelmingly young and male workforce was a cocktail for hilarity and, at times, for mayhem. No one contributed more to the laughter than Paul Byrne of TV3. Blessed, or should that be cursed, by a wicked sense of humour, Paul contributed to some of the most-told stories about pirate radio, as well as some of its most nerve-jangling practical jokes.

'I loved practical jokes – I still do. And it was part and parcel of the whole scene then that you'd get your fair share of them,' he explained. 'I think the news readers probably got most of the practical jokes because they had the "serious" work to do and we were determined to try to put them off.'

'Once, Rob Allen was about to start reading the news bulletin. That was in SouthCoast when they were based on North Main Street. I was hanging around the studio and I spotted a newspaper lying nearby and I couldn't resist it – I put a match to it and put it underneath Rob as he was trying to read the news. In fairness to Rob, his seat was smoking and his ass was probably scorched but he kept reading the news without a break.

'A famous one was to wait until the newsreader was just about to start with the bulletin and to turn the light off in the studio. They'd be trying to read the news from memory or else desperately scrambling for a cigarette lighter to give them enough light to read from their script,' Paul recalled. Some savvy newsreaders even started bringing small torches into the studio with them.

But it was the station managers who were the butt of the worst jokes. They were faced with stations which had been set up from scratch, with a youthful cast of DJs and hangers-on and little or no station experience or rules to fall back on. Several tried to impose office or factory discipline and the result, at times, was utter chaos.

'Michael O'Brien was the main man in SouthCoast when I was there,' Paul explained. 'If I'm honest, I made his life absolute hell. He was a very serious man, a lovely guy and was determined to run the station along set lines. We had the greatest of respect for each other at the end of the day but I loved nothing better than winding Michael up.

'He was a very religious man and he insisted on a "No Play" list for songs he disapproved of. Any song that had a sexual connotation to it was banned. Frankie Goes To Hollywood, Madonna and a load of other artists had songs on the banned list. He was so intent on it that we weren't even allowed play joke songs that had even the remotest sexual hint such as Denise LaSalle's big hit, "Don't Mess With My Toot Toot". I think that was a hit in 1985.

'One day I rang Michael at home and asked him to listen to the radio after the 3 p.m. news bulletin. I think I played three songs from the "No Play" list one after the other, including Denise LaSalle. He jumped into his car and stormed straight to the studio. He ran in shouting at me: "Get out, get out, get out." I laughed and said: "Grand – but who is going to do the rest of the slot?" So I managed to stay on.'

Sometimes the DJs found themselves the victims of dreaded Cork wit. Romano Macari was broadcasting during the Cork 800 celebrations in 1985 with SouthCoast. Jack Lyons was working in the An Post sorting office and listening to Romano when the DJ came up with the concept of properly marking Cork's anniversary by helping to create 800 jobs for local people.

'It became a bit of an item because people liked the idea of it,' Jack recalled. 'Romano was on air and this fella rang in. He was put on air and said that he'd got a job. Romano said it was great and asked him what kind of job? The fella strung him along for a few more questions before he sprang on him that what he had actually received was a blow job.

'There must have been at least four or five seconds of total silence on air. It was absolutely hilarious and it was compelling listening. That is what made pirate radio so special.'

Fergal Barry of SouthCoast admitted that what happened in pirate stations back then would never be tolerated in commercial stations today. But the friendships forged between DJs and staff in the 1970s and 1980s remain to this day. 'I used to read the news bulletins and working with Paul Byrne meant you had to have eyes in the back of your head. He was always trying to make me laugh.

'I remember one particular day a story broke where a man jumped over a wall while trying to run away from the RUC in Northern Ireland. However, what the poor guy didn't realise was that there was a twenty-foot drop on the other side of the wall.

'I was in the studio and suddenly Paul started making a dramatic shadow theatre re-enactment of the entire episode. He was very funny and I started to crack up. But someone had died and it was something that required decorum so it was one of the times that I just had to turn away from the microphone to try to compose myself before continuing with the bulletin.'

Sometimes the joke wasn't intended to be a joke at all. Nick Richards of 96FM recalled his first introduction to Cork pirate radio as a learning curve of Mount Everest-type proportions. 'I flew into Cork from the UK one Thursday at lunchtime. I didn't have a job to go to though I knew there was a pirate radio station in Cork.

'There was a guy working on SouthCoast called Keith York and he met me at the airport. I was wearing a new suit and shiny shoes hoping to land a job and the first thing Keith did was take me to a pig farm where the transmitter was located. Within twenty minutes of landing I was covered in mud and shite – it was on my pants, my shoes, the lot. That was my first introduction to Cork radio.

In the early days of pirate radio, the humour was derived from the all-consuming fear of the Gardaí and the Department of Posts and Telegraphs. One DJ recalled that, on arriving to work at the 'secret' studio just off Wellington Road, he had to climb up a wall and in through a window just to get access to the studio to start his show because the front door was nailed shut to try and protect station personnel from a dreaded raid.

In other cases, the humour was definitely of the juvenile variety. A favourite trick in CCLR, SouthCoast and CBC was to target newcomers, particularly if they were thought to have any notions about themselves. There were two tricks used, both of which were also used in *The Cork Examiner* and *The Evening Echo*, to test new staff.

The first involved leaving a telephone number with a request for the person to call 'Jack Russell' who had been looking to talk to them and a request. The number was for the Cork Society for the Prevention of Cruelty to Animals home. The second similar trick was for a reporter or DJ to be asked to call 'Myra Maynes' at a specific number. When the number was dialled, the unfortunate caller found themselves talking to a receptionist at the Cork Morgue and asking to speak to 'My Remains'.

The stations also targeted each other. It wasn't unusual for an established pirate station like CBC, CCLR or ABC to take umbrage at the pretensions of a newly launched rival like Capitol, Leeside, SouthCoast or even ERI. DJs on the older stations would pick on the worst broadcaster with the new station, ring them up, pretend to be a listener and load them with compliments about how good they were and how much their programme was enjoyed. They'd then ask for a particularly dreadful single to be played as a request – and the unfortunate DJ, having had their ego stroked, felt obliged to play it.

Pearse McCarthy, aka Mark Evans, now a newsreader with 96FM, admitted it was a magical time to be involved in radio. Pearse ended up with a show aged just thirteen – and reckons he has the record for the youngest person on pirate radio. 'Radio was a huge thing for us. I used to listen to BBC, Radio Caroline and Radio Luxembourg. At the time in Ireland all we had was RTÉ Radio 1 and, to be honest, it just didn't suit youngsters.

'I remember the first SouthCoast that set up, I think it was in the Metropole Hotel, it was set up by Pete O'Neill and I remember all these fantastic English DJs – guys like Keith York, Don Stevens and Nick Richards. I remember having listened to Nick on Radio Caroline, so it was incredible.

'I was thirteen and I was already a pirate radio anorak. I contacted the late, great Michael O'Brien who was the station manager and I said I wanted to be involved. I told him I would do anything – answer the phones, take requests, anything. I didn't want money, I just wanted to be involved.

'There was such a sense of romanticism attached to it. It was different radio – you had all these slick jingles, you had all your favourite music that you weren't getting anywhere else. Remember that radio wasn't as public then as it is now – you had all these mysterious DJs who you never got to see. It all added to the mystique of the thing.

'But the guys I met back then – Ken Tobin, Nick Richards, Paul Byrne – are all friends today, thirty years on. But some of the stories I heard back then as a thirteen-year-old were incredible. Some of those English guys had been involved in radio in Israel and all over Europe. Some of the shenanigans – it is only when you are older and you look back and realise that they weren't really sweeter than sweet, they were just mad.

'But my abiding and funniest memory was when the lads in SouthCoast decided to try and raise an aerial on North Main Street. Ken Tobin and Paul Byrne were involved, as they always were. They wanted to raise the aerial to get a better signal but they put it on to the side of the bank. They were doing this at 6 a.m. and of course it attracted attention. The Gardaí arrived, the whole thing had to be taken down and put on another building. At the time I think everyone thought someone was going to get arrested.'

Radio also proved a magnet for characters. Chief amongst them was the late, great Vincent Hanley. A native of Clonmel, he was just thirty-three when he died of an AIDS-related illness in 1987, robbing Ireland of one of the most talented broadcasters the country has ever produced. He has since been described as Ireland's first gay celebrity. Nicknamed 'Fab Vinny', he arrived on Cork's radio and disco scene like a meteor in the late 1970s. Those who knew him at the time, including Stevie Bolger, recognised instantly he was destined for great things. Despite boasting many friends within Cork's pirate stations, Vincent Hanley never actually worked for any of the Cork pirates.

'He was astonishing – it was as if he was born to operate behind a microphone. My God but he was absolutely brilliant. I knew he was going to the very top and it was such a terrible tragedy that he died so young. I don't think anyone who saw him in Cork clubs at the time could ever forget him,' Stevie recalled.

'Fab Vinny' brought a sense of the exotic with him. 'One day, he asked me to go across to Cash's (now Brown Thomas) with him. I didn't mind in the slightest because the girls working in Cash's were absolutely gorgeous and no one needed an excuse to go in and admire them. In we walked and Vinny was straight over to the counter asking to try moisturisers and lotions and potions. The girls were entranced by him. It was something you didn't see every day in Cork at the time.'

For others, it was less a case of the lotions and potions in Cash's than trying hard not to get hypothermia in the studio. Colin Noone, aka Colin Edwards, started with Radio Caroline and said the studio, located in a caravan in Togher, would get so cold in winter that DJs would struggle to set up records with frozen fingers. 'It was absolutely freezing in wintertime. I will never forget one winter's day out there. It was really windy. I was on the air and the AM aerial used to be a piece of wire – it would run from the back of the caravan, onto a branch and then across the road and up a tree. It was a hundred-foot wire and, needless to say, it wasn't put up properly. It was so windy the wire was being lashed around outside and the No. 14 bus passed, hooked on to the wire as it blew and then dragged the whole thing away. We lost all AM listeners for a couple of days.

'I went from Radio Caroline to SouthCoast thanks to Don Stevens and Keith York. From there, after a bit of a gap, I went to the revived SouthCoast. I ended up with 96FM for about a year and a half but I couldn't handle it because I was told what to say, what to play and then the computer would play it. You'd find yourself sitting there and waiting for the computer to tell you it was OK to talk. To me, that is not radio.

'But I'm so delighted to see so many of the "old heads" from that time still doing so well. People like Rob Allen, Trevor Welch, PJ Coogan, Ken Tobin and Paul Byrne. Mind you, Paul Byrne was mad – but he was such a great laugh to work with. A great guy.

'There were almost always parties going on in the studios. We were all friends and we used to hang out together. It was the most natural thing in the world to head into the studio during a night out – it didn't matter that you wouldn't have a show that night. You'd go in and meet the lads, have a laugh and a bit of craic.'

Ken Regis of CCLR and De Lacy House said pirate stations were magical places to work at the time. 'I love music but I can't sing and I can't play an instrument. So the only way I was ever going to be involved in music was through presentation. I said: "Hey, why not be a DJ?" And that is what got me into it.

'I'm with LMFM Radio now up in Drogheda. Talk about having the dream gig! I love the music of the 1970s and 1980s.

And what show do I have now? Playing the hits of the 1980s. I never left my cocoon of playing the music of the 1980s. I started playing the great songs of that era and I'm still doing it today. What a great job.'

Jim Collins, aka Dave Stewart, of ABC said the sense of fun was aided by the impromptu manner in which shows were prepared. Sometimes, detailed preparation wasn't what was required. 'I had a week to prepare for my first show on ABC and I worked really hard for it. I was very careful. I wrote everything down – what I was going to say, the songs I was going to play, etc. I asked my friend Jim Gibbons what he thought afterwards and he said it sounded as if I was reading everything out from a piece of paper. I told him I actually was reading it out and we moved on from there.'

Ian Richards of CCLR and Capitol Radio said friendship and humour were always at the core of Cork's pirate stations. 'I was home from Holland when I got a phone call from Pat Goggin who was station manager in Capitol Radio. It was around Christmas and Pat needed help over the holidays with some of the afternoon slots because of people being away. The studio was over the Pickin' Chicken in the city centre and I enjoyed it so much that I never went back to Holland.

'I was there for a couple of years and it was great fun. One of the lads used to test the power of the transmitter by holding his hand up close to it and seeing how far the sparks would jump. The greater the distance it could jump, the greater the power of the transmission. I don't think people realise what a joy Cork is to live in now. Back then, it was a depressing place with all the unemployment and the industries closing down. Maybe that is why people have such fond memories of pirate radio stations, because they brought a little laughter into people's lives just when they needed it most.'

Stevie Bolger recalled that it helped if you were a bit mad. 'Con McParland was involved with DJ Daniels and myself in CBC. He was the technical brains – if you can call it that – behind the station and he was the one always checking the broadcasting gear. I will never forget the sight of him holding a fluorescent tube and walking over to the transmitter. You could check the strength of the signal by how the tube started glowing depending on how close you were to the transmitter. He never seemed to be happy with the thing and would then start soldering to get a better, more powerful signal. It's a wonder none of us are still glowing in the dark to this day.'

CHAPTER THIRTEEN

PJ Coogan, aka Tony Black: 'I was a noisy child and, to shut me up, my mother used to turn on the radio. That was my earliest memory of pirate radio. She used to put on the old RTÉ Radio 1 shows and I grew up listening to music. Then it was Radio Luxembourg and I remember discovering music to the left or right, whatever way you want to phrase it, of what RTÉ were playing.

'I will always remember hearing the voice of the great Tony Adams and then later discovering that there were radio stations in Cork. I think CBC was the first pirate station I listened to. Some of them were great but, in fairness, some of them were awful too.

'This would have been in the late 1970s. The one thing I remember doing – the same thing every other teen did at the time – was sitting at home and taping music from the radio. I'd listen to Derry O'Callaghan's show and what I liked was that while Larry Gogan on 2FM would play the hits and talk over the end of the songs, Derry would stay quiet until the song was finished, so you'd get a very good quality tape.

'I thought that was really professional broadcasting, but what I realise now was that Derry was probably making himself a cup of coffee or had run out to the loo. Larry Gogan had people to make his coffee for him in RTÉ. But I did listen to ABC, CBC and the smaller stations like Radio Caroline. There were great jocks like DJ Daniels and people like that.

'It was a huge thing to discover as a teen that you had radio stations that played music all night long. This was way before multichannel TV, computer games or the Internet. Music and sport was our life so to discover that you could listen to pop and rock music all night long was like discovering a hoard of gold.

'Music was everything to me – I remember listening to Radio Luxembourg and being amazed by the music. I'd sit at home with a hairbrush and pretend to be a DJ working for Radio Luxembourg. I got a stereo one Christmas and there was a tape deck in it. I'd put on my headphones, introduce the music and talk to myself. I would do that in my bedroom for an hour after school and it was imagination run riot. I would listen to the real Radio Luxembourg at night and, over time, I suddenly realised that I could do that too.

'About 1983 I went up to St Luke's one afternoon and I knocked on the door of SouthCoast and asked to be shown around. I will always remember who was there that day – Don Stevens, the great Pete O'Neill and Tony Allen. Tony was just being Tony, the genius that he was. He didn't deliberately try to shatter my illusions but he told me you didn't need an English accent to be on radio.

'My first appearance on pirate radio was on John Kenny's 'Other Side of the Fence' show on a Thursday night. They would bring in a member of the listening audience to review the music releases of the week. I will always remember the release that came out on top that week – Darryl Hall and John Oates. I thought it was awful but it went on to reach No. 1. Needless to say I was never asked back on again.

'Around September 1984 I was in college doing a science course and listening to Radio Caroline. I was listening to Don

Hynes, aka Donal McKeown, and a few others and again thought to myself: "I can do that." I went out and found the station, which wasn't hard since it was a caravan in the garden of a house. I knocked on the door and it was opened by a guy who would become one of my dearest friends, Ken Tobin.

'Ken was about sixteen at the time. I was brought in and introduced to Mickey Daly and his mother. I said, "I want to be on the radio." He told me I needed a demo tape and a CV. I put a tape together, no problem. His mother gave me tea and buns while Mickey told me I was very inexperienced. But Cork were playing in a football match that Sunday and the phone rang at 7 p.m. on the Saturday night. My mother took the call and told me a fella called Michael Daly was looking for me. I took the phone and Mickey said he wanted to watch the Cork match and asked could I do the 4 p.m. to 6 p.m. slot? That was my break.

'As far as I was concerned, I was a total disaster during that first show. But Mickey seemed happy and I was asked back. I still remember the first record I played was by Freddie Mercury. Mickey later asked me could I do an hour in the mornings from 10 a.m. to 11 a.m. I looked at my college lecture schedule and thought I can do that. A couple of Sundays later, I was asked to start at 3 p.m. and I was told a very special DJ was starting work for Radio Caroline. Mickey Daly said it was Kid Jensen's younger brother, Scott. I soon realised it was Trevor Welch from Togher, who was no more a brother to the BBC DJ than I was to Freddie Mercury.

'Radio Caroline was a great place but the studio was hilarious. There were two turntables balanced either side of a table and there was a couple of milk crates balanced on bricks in the caravan with a hole cut in a wooden door for access. It was the most precarious thing I'd ever seen. The microphone basically had a foam stuck on it, which was a kitchen cleaner with the scouring end cut off with a scissors. It was an ultra-modern American-style studio so we were told.

'I went from knowing I *wanted* to do radio to suddenly discovering that I *could* do the work. And I worked very, very hard to ensure that I did it well. I then decided I wanted to work in a proper studio with proper gear. Myself and Ken Tobin used to do the Saturday afternoon show and we did the sports results. We always announced that the sports results were broadcast from Radio Caroline's studio two. That was me plugging a microphone into the mixing deck and going down to the kitchenette at the other end of the caravan and going through the football scores. The kitchenette had a nice little echo and it did sound as if you were somewhere else other than the main studio.

'I heard while I was working with Radio Caroline that there was a new SouthCoast about to start up. It was up over a chicken restaurant on North Main Street. I was told the man to see was 'Shaky' O'Brien. I had a tape of my stuff and I gave it to him. He said: 'Yeah, fine – I have a slot for you.' I went back to Mickey and said SouthCoast wanted me. I thanked him for all he had done for me but he gave out to me and said I was full of shite and wouldn't amount to anything.

'SouthCoast had what we never had which was a record collection. It was just boxes piled on the floor but they had fantastic stuff. I was doing late nights, early mornings or whatever was needed. I was doing gigs to make a few bob and then, after a time, it began to get semi-professional. The equipment started to get better and the studio was suddenly properly wired together.

'But everyone was still very cautious because the pirate stations were still illegal. We had moved into a new building and there were offices in the front and the studios to the rear. There was a guy putting a phone line in and he asked if one of the DJs could play a request for his wife. Shaky immediately wanted to know how he had sussed out that the offices were linked to SouthCoast Radio? The guy just pointed and, above a door to the rear of the building, someone had put up a banner which read "Welcome to SouthCoast Radio".

'My father was a garda and he thought I would grow out of this fascination with radio. But my poor mother wasn't too pleased. Quite predictably, given the amount of time I was spending on air, I failed my college exams. I told my family I was taking a year off and I did exams only, which you could do in college at the time. I passed them and she was horrified because I then started doing a full-time radio show.

'I was playing discos four or five nights a week. There was some money from the gigs but very little from the pirate radio stuff. You might get a few quid, maybe IR£10 or so, on a Friday night and you could go to Maudie Whelan's pub on North Main Street for a few pints and a game of snooker.

'I had a decent record collection, I knew John Barry and he sorted me with a few gigs. I did well enough at them and that led to more gigs. Dermot Brady was an old friend of my father's and I went to him asking if he could give me a gig in his Grand Parade hotel. He did and I started out playing there once every fortnight but it ended up that I was playing there four nights a week.

'I never went back to college after passing my yearly exams. It probably wasn't the right thing to do. But I loved what I was doing, I was making out OK financially at it and I thought, why change?

'There were great people involved in the whole thing and I was learning a lot. Bob Stokes was involved and some of us thought he was like a God in radio just because he had a Dublin accent. For a time you thought all the clever people had to have an English or a Dublin accent in radio. But then you realised that there was a huge pool of talent in Cork itself.

'I worked for Radio Caroline, then SouthCoast and even WBEN. I talked my way past Neil Francis, a Dublin director, and had a gig there. They had beautiful studios just over a Chinese restaurant and across the road from Rocky's (restaurant). Literally the day before I was due to start they got raided and Romano Macari rang me and sent a taxi to get me. He brought me out to the caravan they were suddenly operating from now and I thought: "Here we go again." It was a music-based station and you spoke maybe three times in an hour? It was great and the music was absolutely brilliant.

'It was hilarious. There was this caravan in the middle of a muddy field with a guard dog tied up at the rear. I got covered in mud just getting to the caravan. I was doing an early morning gig and, around 9 a.m. or so, I thought I'd better pull the curtains and see what was going on. I almost shit myself because, when I pulled the curtains, there was this bullock staring in the window at me. Romano said it was only for a few days until we got to a new studio in town.

'But the holy grail for us all was ERI. It was the big station. They had a great set-up and wonderful studios. In 1988 I got a tape to them and Margaret O'Connor gave me an overnight shift on the station. I was just playing records, there was no talking. Three weeks into that I got one talking shift and then I got a call from Lucia Proctor in RTÉ to whom I had applied about eighteen months before. They had a once in a fortnight slot, twenty-five minutes long, on a Cork link to Maxi's programme on 2FM. I took it. They paid me IR£70 for that twenty-five minute slot, which involved maybe over an hour's work. I never got IR£70 for a week's work in pirate radio let alone for one single gig.

'I had to ring Margaret and explain what happened. I always remember what she said to me: "Ah well, I had plans for you. But RTÉ is where we all want to go." We didn't fall out over it and we are friends to this day. I met her at the radio awards just a short time back. She still maintains I made a big mistake and should have stuck with ERI. She reckons if I had stayed with the pirates and grown within the industry I would have done better in later years.

'With RTÉ I found myself jobbing around the place. I was working out of Cork RTÉ on Union Quay for four years from 1989. I used to cover for Stevie Bolger. I tried to cover for others and I did Sunday mornings for Maxi. I also did a show called *New Voices* which was four Saturdays in a row. It was a magnificent radio show and I learned so much. Then, as the new stations were coming on board, I moved again. I was in RTÉ before the old pirates started to shut down. The changeover wasn't handled well. Radio South opened in August 1989 and all the people that had helped build the Cork pirate stations into seriously heavy hitters were let go. It was a big mistake by the directors of the new licensed commercial stations to turn their backs on so many of the old pirate radio officials.

'My memory of 96FM back then was the Australian radio experts who came in. They took one look at what we were doing and said: "Guys, this has to stop and stop now or you'll all be out of a job by Christmas. You are wasting your time with this kind of stuff." They brought in a more rigid format that was geared towards market share and commercial realities. It was far more rigid than anything pirate radio had ever seen. They told us to stick with it and it would work. It did and that largely underpinned the strength of 96FM that you see today.

'Unfortunately, radio today is all about the figures. It is a good thing commercially but a bad thing professionally. I loved the sense of freedom and adventure that was in the pirate stations. But commercial realities ultimately rule over everything, though I suppose it is true to say that it is not as much fun as it used to be. Radio can be rigid today and I do feel sorry for up-and-coming young Irish entertainers and bands because it is so hard now to get stuff played. That wouldn't have happened back in 1985.

'Chris Rea has gone on record saying that Irish pirate radio saved his career. We played his music when other established stations wouldn't. That made him a star in Ireland and helped kick-start his career back in the UK again. That's why he recorded the album *Shamrock Diaries* to put on record his gratitude to Ireland for giving him back his career.

'Radio stations are a tremendous melting pot. No two stations are the same and no two jocks are the same in terms of presentation styles and musical tastes. There was a great crew involved in pirate radio in Cork at that time. People were very decent to one another and I made friends back then that I still call friends today. I think you can read a lot into the fact that most of us working in pirate radio weren't getting paid much, if at all. It was for the love of music that we all got involved.

'You also knew the guys that were going to make it big. John Creedon was exceptional and Tony Allen was incredible. Tony was the most gifted all-round broadcaster I have ever come across. It is a pity he is not alive for this book because he would fill half the chapters himself with stories. Tony was a lunatic and he was a genius. In Cook Street he took me under his wing and we were friends for the year while we were there together. I learned things from Tony that I am still using today over twenty years later, that's how good he was.

'Back in the mid 1980s I was more or less gigging professionally as a DJ. I had gigs four or five nights a week and was making really good money. I had the breakfast show on WBEN from 7 a.m. to 11.30 a.m., I would go home and get a couple of hours sleep and then it was in to The Grand Parade Hotel. You'd finish at 5 a.m. or so, grab an hour's sleep and then head back in to the radio station for the morning show.

'There was massive money being earned. I was getting maybe IR£150 a week between radio and the various DJ gigs. It was stupid money and two and three times what guys were earning in other jobs. I remember getting IR£500 for DJ work over the Guinness Jazz Festival weekend back in the late 1980s. If you worked hard and scored a lot of DJ gigs, you weren't too worried about making money from pirate radio because you were set up OK.'

CHAPTER FOURTEEN

Ken Tobin, aka Steve Davis: 'The earliest radio memory for me was listening to stations like Capital Radio, Radio City, CBC and it was something that was just unbelievable. Every time I listened to pirate radio I got excited and thought to myself that I want to be part of it.

'I was about fifteen years old and one of my first engagements with pirate radio was when I wrote to Radio City, to a guy called Eric Hansen, and told him I was interested in radio and would love to be part of it.

'I was invited in to the radio station and one of the first records I ever introduced on air – I was only at the station for about an hour – was The Nick Straker Band's "A Walk In The Park". It must have been around 1980. I knew then that it was all I wanted to do. Nothing else – I wanted to be part of radio. That guy Eric Hansen, funny enough, people might know him today as John Creedon.

'I loved music. But there wasn't a lot of scope at the time on radio for anyone who loved pop music or liked listening to music. You had RTÉ Radio 1 (2FM wasn't even on the air at that point) but that was it. I remember being up in my bedroom and Radio Luxembourg would come on at 7 p.m. in the evening and you would listen to the Top 40. That's where I would hear the kind of music that I wanted to listen to. People like Benny Brown, *Back in Town*. These DJs were fantastic. There was absolutely nothing like that in Ireland at the time. That is why I really wanted to be involved in radio. There was an excitement about it.

'My first proper involvement in pirate radio was a station based in Togher called Radio Caroline. I'm from Togher and I lived in Togher so that's how it came about. I started asking questions. This would have been in the very early 1980s. I was asking people about the station. Did people know where it broadcast from? Did they know the DJ? Guys my age interested in sport and football, just like me, they looked at me kind of funny because I was asking about pirate radio stations that they didn't know a whole lot about.

'I remember standing outside a flat in Togher after it was pointed out to me that someone thought the radio station broadcast from that house. I just looked at this flat and the people going into it. I was in awe – I was that close to pirate radio. I wanted to be in there but I didn't have the balls at the time to just walk in and ask.

'So I asked around and I got to know the guy who moved the radio station from there further out into Togher. Mickey Daly was his name. I went out, introduced myself and before I knew it I had my first radio show which was in a caravan at the back of this guy's house.

'I thought when I left there that it would be the last caravan I would ever broadcast from. But it wasn't. There was another one, WBEN, up on the northside which also operated from a caravan. It was in a farm overlooking the city. We had to go through a cow shed. I was on one night, there was a security guard there – I cannot remember his name to this day – who had a great sense of humour. You had to go through the cow shed to get to the caravan where we broadcast from. He would be there with his flash light to guide us through the cow shed and, just for a laugh, he'd turn it off half way through. All you'd hear would be the cows and the rats rustling in the straw. You'd give him a dig or a kick and shout "turn it on". He'd turn it on and you'd see the rats scatter from the light. This is what we did – this was the fame and glamour of pirate radio.

'If memory serves me correct, WBEN moved from the city centre to a caravan up on the northside before it ended up back in the city centre again. The things you had to go through just to get on the air. It was unbelievable.

'The radio station all depended on the person who opened it. It all depended on the money that was available and how serious they were about the station. I mean, in Cork you have the likes of CCLR, Radio City – not very big budgets. But then you had the super pirates that came on the air, the SouthCoast Radios, the ERIs. When you saw the studios that they operated from, it was an eye-opener.

'ERI had the first purpose-built radio station in Ireland. They gutted the house out completely, stuck in a studio, stuck in production units and offices upstairs. It was a new direction they were going in. Both SouthCoast and ERI thought it was possible. Before that, CCLR went off the air on the Friday night before I was scheduled to start with them.

'I was due to do a gig with them on the Saturday and they went off the air on the Friday. I remember all my friends were heading off for the weekend, it was a beautiful summer's weekend, and here was I staying behind. But when I heard the station wasn't on the air I headed off to join the lads at Owenahincha. On the Monday, I went in to the owner, I think his name was O'Shea, and he told me I missed the Saturday night slot. I said they weren't on the air but he said they went off the air on Friday but were back on the following evening and I wasn't there. He said: "That's it, sorry, you are finished." So I was fired before I even started.

'The pirate radio station studio was your deck, your mixer and your phone. That was basically it – you brought your own records with you. But you were there for the music. The rest of the stuff didn't really matter.

'You chose your own music. There was no such thing as agreed playlists or strategies. Basically, you were a cool DJ if you had your own record box and people spotted you walking across the street with your record box and your headphones hanging off it.

'You loved that people knew it. There was something cool about being a pirate radio DJ. I worked for Cork Co. Council many, many years ago. I was building a wall out in Grange in Douglas and when I finished on a Friday I went straight home and I had a list of records I had written out for my mother. She would go into town the following day and buy those records for me. I had to work so I couldn't go into town myself. I would give her "x" amount of money to buy them and I can tell you I couldn't wait to come home from work that evening and go up into my bedroom and put those singles or 45s onto the deck and listen to them.

'That is what you did and that is how you sorted out what you were going to play. If you liked a single, you made sure to play it the next time you were on air. You spent every penny you had on records and I think that love of music came through on air.

'Like all DJs, I had to have a broadcast name or a "handle" if you like. Because we were pirate radio stations and, I suppose, illegal in terms of our broadcasting, you didn't use your own name.

'As far as I can remember I went with the name Steve Davis because I thought it was a warm and friendly name. That's how I wanted to be seen on the radio. Not as someone who was big-headed or who wanted to be famous. I wanted to be friendly and it helped that I was a snooker fan.

'Two people that had a huge influence on me when I was in pirate radio are actually no longer with us. Donie McKeown was one of them and he worked on Radio Caroline in Togher. This guy was unbelievable. He had the gift of the gab and he loved a pint. He also loved his music. He was, to the best of my knowledge, one of the first that ever did one of those *Oldies and Irish* kind of shows. He played Irish music and also gave a bit of time to Frank Sinatra, Perry Como and other greats. Donie was such a nice fella and the banter on his show was incredible. He was such a nice guy that he often went to meet the people that would ring up to compliment or ask questions about his show.

'Donie one day had a competition in a pub he was having a drink in somewhere in town. He would make a few bob for himself whereby he would start a book in the pub about the person on air at the time. Say it was me, Ken Tobin, and he would take bets on how old I was. He'd charge them to guess how old I was. Then he'd bring me into the pub a few weeks later to settle the bet. But he would warn me going in the door not to ask for a drink because I was only sixteen and he knew the owner wouldn't serve me. But I had to go in to verify how old I was and to present the winner with his money.

'Radio, not just pirate radio, has been huge for me. It is a major part of my life. It is how I make my living and it is what I always wanted to do as a young person. I tell people that working on a pirate radio station was a bit like a FÁS course. When you went in you started learning about the business –

how it worked, how to make money, how to present, how to chose music. You also got to be surrounded by people that loved radio. That was how it was back in the 1970s and 1980s. That is how it still is today.

'If I was to estimate it, I would say that 99.5 per cent of people involved in radio today came up through the pirate stations in the 1970s and 1980s. That says an awful lot about the people, the era and the love for radio. I went for my legal job, if you like, with radio when the licenses were awarded in 1989 and most of the people in the room when I walked in that day were people that I had worked alongside in pirate stations.

'They were hugely influential. To tell the truth, there would be no independent radio industry in Ireland today if it wasn't for the pirates. The quality of broadcasting wouldn't be as good as it is. That is how important it was.

'Cork was a real hotbed for pirate stations. There were times in the 1980s when you had between five and seven pirate stations all on the air at the same time. It was unbelievable – you could go along the wavelength band and you'd have Capital Radio, CCLR, Radio City and Radio Caroline. They were all on the air at the time. It was a hugely exciting time in Cork. It was absolutely fantastic.

'It was like any other business in ways. People tuned up their presenting techniques and got to be more relaxed behind the microphone. The first time you went into a radio station you were excited and nervous. But, as time went on, you got better and you really settled into the station and your show.

'You could actually map the way things were changing. The standards went up, people got better at what they did and the stations began to spend a bit more to improve how they worked. It got a lot more professional. It was a clique, in a way, where this group of people in Cork loved music and worked in both radio and in discos. Everybody knew everybody else – if there was work going in a club, you were told about it. If a guy had a gig in Spiders and he knew there was a slot free in Chandras, he would ring up a friend in pirate radio and tell him about it.

'In my case, it was De Lacy House but there was also a club down Caroline Street called Swingers. If you look at De Lacy House, they had Paul Byrne (TV3), Trevor Welch (TV3/Setanta), myself and loads of others. We were all honing our skills. We all worked in that caravan out in Togher, as did PJ Coogan (now 96FM).

'Nightclubs were how we all survived. Pirate radio just didn't pay. But playing discos and nightclubs gave us an income and supplemented our love for pirate radio. That is how we made our money.

'I dreamed about working in radio. There was nothing else I wanted to do. It is funny, because people's attitude towards radio back then was unbelievable. When you think about it in today's terms it is incredible. I was just sixteen when I walked into pirate radio. I had no interest in school – none. I loved playing football and the GAA. But radio was my goal.

'I sat down with my parents and said this is what I wanted to do: I want to work in pirate radio. They were very naive, I suppose, because one of the first things they asked was how I was going to survive given that there wasn't much money in pirate radio. Secondly, they said, and this is the funny side of it, I would not make it on radio. I asked them why I shouldn't have a chance like everyone else? They told me I wouldn't make it because I didn't speak Irish. That was their reckoning – if you didn't speak Irish you would never work for Radio Éireann, as RTÉ was known as then.

'It sounded silly to me at the time and, I suppose looking back on it now, it was very silly. I saw the pirates as exciting and the place to be. That's where I wanted to work and I have never regretted it for a single second.

'I've spent my entire radio career in Cork. I've spent one week outside Cork working on a pirate radio station and that was in Galway with a station called Atlantic Sound. I lasted one week. I enjoyed the week but, on the Friday, I was handed an envelope with IR £20 inside in it. I was expected to survive for another week on that. Because it was a new city to me, I didn't have any disco or nightclub gigs to fall back on so that was it. The guy told me: "Look, if we make it, you make it." But I told the guy who brought me up there, John Fullam, I'm going back to Cork.

'I grew up loving Capitol Radio, which was based in Tuckey Street, directly over where Pat Grace's Fried Chicken is now. There was a guy called Johnny Gaynor and I never missed his show. He had an English accent and he did the drive-time show. That's one of the reasons I fell in love with radio and, at the time, I just wanted to be Johnny Gaynor.

'Part of the problem, in the early 1980s, was the perception that being professional for a Cork pirate radio station meant having DJs and presenters who were from Dublin or the UK. It was a problem that threatened to wreck the dreams of an aspiring army of young Cork-born radio stars.

'Peter O'Neill is a guy that had a huge influence on not just my career but I think the careers of a lot of the lads that came up through pirate radio in the 1980s. I remember going up to SouthCoast which was the super pirate radio station of the time. They were up in St Luke's and Peter had this idea where he wanted local jocks to do work at the weekends.

'The weekday Monday to Friday jobs would go to guys who came down from Dublin or over to Cork from England. They were very professional because of the work they had done in Dublin, England or even Northern Ireland. The idea was to give local guys a chance at the weekends so they could build experience. I remember one of the guys involved in financing the station, the late Michael O'Brien, was talking to Pete and the plan was being explained to him.

'I was standing next to Pete and I was saying to myself: "Yes, this is it – my big break." But Michael O'Brien said "No, it ain't happening." He felt it was a professionally run radio station and he wanted to use the jocks that they had. He felt the local lads weren't ready yet. I remember having the argument with him and then joking with him years later when I was on 96FM that he had stopped me working on SouthCoast Radio.'

CHAPTER FIFTEEN

Don Walsh, aka DJ Daniels, aka Dave Porter: 'CBC was the first pirate radio station that I had any dealings with. In fact, that station was basically Stevie Bolger, Con McParland and myself. We started in the small front bedroom of my mother's house at Wilton Gardens. Con McParland was the technical genius, and a very clever bloke he was. But, in my book, he was like a lot of other very clever people and ranked as a borderline lunatic. We did stuff together back then that Health and Safety Authority officials would have a fit about today. For instance, putting aerials up by climbing along the roofs of five-storey buildings up in St Luke's without a harness – that kind of thing.

'This would have been in the late 1970s and I suppose a lot of what we were doing was groundbreaking. At that time your radio choice was RTÉ or RTÉ. As young whippersnappers we wanted to listen to the music we liked and that just wasn't being played by RTÉ. I was very much involved in the music scene, as was Stevie. We both knew what was happening in the UK with music radio and we thought what was happening in Ireland was balderdash by comparison.

'We said we would give it a try ourselves and that is what we did in Cork with CBC. I don't remember precisely how it ended up being the three of us but we set up the station and started broadcasting within a couple of weeks of deciding to do so. The draw for me was that I was a DJ and I wanted to try to do here in Ireland what DJs were doing across the water in the UK. You had stuff like Radio Caroline happening in the UK and it was all really exciting.

'I was playing as a DJ in clubs for a younger audience who kept complaining that they weren't being catered for by RTÉ. This was well before 2FM remember. So we decided to give CBC a go – and, to be honest, finance never really came into it. We set it up as much for our own pleasure. We certainly never saw it as a purely profit-making venture.

'I came from a normal working-class background. I was brought up just across the road from Jackie Lennox's fish and chip shop. I was one of nine children and we came in batches of three. The first three were married and out the door before I arrived at school age. I grew up with six of us in the house, which had a retail shop attached to it. I had incredible parents, they both worked very hard so that the "Last of the Mohicans" as we called ourselves, my brother Liam, my sister Frances and myself, all got great secondary school educations.

'We saw how hard they worked and I suppose it rubbed off on us. I worked hard all my life, starting out in Jackie Lennox's and then going on to other things. So when we decided to give the radio station a go I was going to work very hard to make sure it didn't embarrass us.

'There was a place called The Hideout in Paul Street and a lot of young people would go there and listen to music. I used to "spin the discs" there and I liked the whole scene. I suppose it was about 1966 and my career path had already been chosen for me. Looking back now I still say that 1968 was one of the greatest years ever for music. You had the start of the whole Motown scene and there was incredible music coming from the UK. I was just starting to work as a DJ and you had places like Good Time Charlies and later places like Chandras, Cocos, Stardust and Krojacks. De Lacy House and Sir Henry's became some of the best places in Cork. The real old-timers will remember The Smokey Sea in Glenbrook – that was Bobby Carpenter's place.

'By the 1970s the old dancehall scene was fading and you had huge interest in things like folk rock, hard rock, glam rock and then the whole disco thing was starting up. People had a bit more money and were spending it on records and better quality radios. It was a huge thing at the time to tune into Radio Luxembourg or Radio Caroline.

'But what probably spoiled the whole CBC thing for us was when advertising revenues started to come into it. It was all great fun when there was no money involved, but then when revenues started coming in, you had to take care of the coin. We never saw it as a commercial operation or something that would give any of us a livelihood. It was all for the craic at the start.

'It was an incredible time. We had a very basic broadcasting unit and, for a time, we were causing havoc with local TV reception. But we were set up on a shoestring budget. There were no proper signal controls or filtrations. We just wanted to reach a Cork audience with our station and we certainly did that. Within a few weeks we started to get a reaction – people were contacting us about requests, asking for certain bands and songs to be played and stuff like that.

'It was real off-the-cuff stuff at the very beginning but, the longer we were on air, the better we got at what we were doing and we began to regulate the station a bit better. We weren't broadcasting 24–7 but we did begin to broadcast over regular time slots so that people knew when to tune in. The buzz and the payback was playing a club as a DJ later and having people come up to you and tell you how much they loved the station and looked forward to tuning in every day.

'My vague recollection is that we once got a phone call from Charleville in north Cork and there was someone there who could listen in to us. Now how in sweet loving Christmas we got our signal that far out is beyond me. Our aim was to cover Cork city and that was it. When we were up in St Luke's we had the height to get pretty good coverage over the city and, I suppose, there were times when the signal would carry quite a distance out into the county.

'It was very high up there in St Luke's. I remember one bitterly cold winter day having to climb out onto the roof and set up an aerial with Con McParland. We were taking risks back then that makes it a miracle we are still around today. But that was the thing with pirate radio – if something had to be done or fixed you had to do it yourself.

'The other amazing thing about CBC was that, shortly after Stevie and myself set it up, we quickly began to attract people who wanted to be DJs. They were people with a similar love of music and, while they didn't have any experience, they more than made up for it with the level of enthusiasm they had. You had Stevie who was a brilliant broadcaster, Henry Condon who was born for radio, John Creedon and a host of others.

'I never considered myself a broadcaster, certainly not a professional broadcaster. I worked as a DJ from about 1966. I got paid for gigs or whatever. But when you started doing radio shows and such, the money for your DJ work became significantly higher. That was the major benefit for me. We had a fantastic and loyal fan base. You had people who would listen to you on radio and then make sure to attend whatever clubs or gigs you were playing at as a DJ.

'CBC began with none of us really knowing what the hell was going on. We literally played it by ear. None of us were savvy about broadcasting or the potential for revenues. It was hit-and-miss for quite a while. For about four weeks we kept at it – I suppose today you would call them pilot shows. But then, about a month or so into it, we began to get a response. People seemed to like CBC and what we were trying to do.

'Our "jingles" came from England. When you were on air for a bit you had radio enthusiasts ringing you up and giving you advice about how to improve and what was going on with other stations. There was a disco sound and lighting supplier in London. We bought stock from them and the "jingles" were included. But we got clever at a later stage and had our own customised "jingles" made up. It helped the station sound very professional.'

'But we still made mistakes. I made the error once of giving out my home phone number on air and my mother went ballistic because the phone never stopped ringing with people wanting to get requests played or talk to the DJs. I went by the nickname "DJ Daniels" and I broadcast just about everything in terms of times, formats and music. I really liked jazz and I was involved in the Cork Jazz Festival. I was lucky to meet a lot of very serious jazz heads and I suppose it was inevitable that I would run a jazz show on CBC.

'I did the show until 11 a.m. on a Sunday morning and the reaction to it was fantastic. I was mixing music with interviews and jazz fans really liked it. What was great was the level of feedback we would get. Because we were playing in clubs, people would give you an honest opinion about what they liked and didn't like. If a lot of people told you they didn't like a particular thing, you would try and do it differently.

'Pirate radio gave me incredible experience. We were effectively the first pirate station in Cork and were hauled into the High Court on a number of occasions. I had a friend who was a solicitor, Rory Conway, and he liked what we were doing and he would nail his colours to the mast and help us out. We got huge publicity from the trips to the High Court and I think we stirred things up sufficiently in Cork. There was only one pirate station in Dublin but then, very quickly, it became like a bun fight with so many new stations starting up.

'Cork people fell in love with pirate radio. The younger generation just weren't going to settle for one RTÉ station which basically ignored their music. At that point in time RTÉ's musical content was pretty staid and boring.

'The end for me came when I got married and moved from Cork to Dublin. It was the end of the 1970s. After that I moved to the UK and that took me out of the Cork music scene altogether. When I moved to the UK in the early 1980s you had ERI and SouthCoast coming on to the scene and they were different animals altogether to what we had with CBC. They became known as the "super pirates" because of their resources compared to what we had just a few years earlier.

'Being involved in CBC was one of the happiest times of my life. I still listen to radio a lot today and the stations I like are the ones that remind me of all the stuff we were playing in the 1970s. The buzz for music and radio is worse than a contagious disease. I'd love to get back behind a turntable again and, if I'm honest, I would give anything to go back to my first love which is jazz. It is not something that I have ever pursued but, who knows, it might still happen for me. That's the amazing part about it – you never stop dreaming.'

CHAPTER SIXTEEN

Stevie Bolger, aka Chris Stevens: 'My adventures in Cork started in the mid 1970s, when I came down from Dublin to work in a new nightclub opening on Caroline Street called "Good Time Charlies". It was my job as Entertainment Manager to book the bands, DJs, and organise promotions for the Dublin and Cork venues.

'I instantly liked Cork. I loved the size and buzz of the city, its people, music, theatre and the clubs. Plus, I believed that Cork had the most beautiful women in Ireland – that's why I married one. So I decided to stay. It has been my home ever since.

'The first time I heard pirate radio was in Dublin. I thought why can't we do this in Cork? On my return to Leeside, I called Don Walsh (DJ Daniels), who had a music shop on MacCurtain Street and could provide the studio equipment. Con McParland was the man to build a transmitter; a most crucial requirement for broadcasting. But Con equally, and most importantly, would be the on-air talent for Cork Broadcasting Company (CBC).

'Those first few weeks and months on air were very exciting. The reaction from listeners and local papers was encouraging. Perhaps we were too popular because it wasn't long before we were raided.'

'Despite the fact that we were illegal operators we decided to challenge the system in the High Court in Dublin. A report in *The Cork Examiner* at the time stated: "Detectives, Gardaí and officials from the Department of Post and Telegraphs raided the radio station's premises in Montenotte and confiscated equipment, including their transmitter, worth IR£3,000." I remember it well.

'Outlining the plaintiff's case, Mr James O'Driscoll, S.C. said the claim was for an injunction to stop the authorities from repeating what they had done the previous day. Equipment had been confiscated under Section 8 of the Wireless Telegraph Act, 1926, and under that section there did not appear to be any remedy to have the equipment returned.

'We lost the challenge on the day. But if we had won our case, it could have been the foundation of commercial radio in this country. Some months later what could be best described as "musical differences" set in among the management at CBC. It was a lot like being in a band with the musicians disagreeing over the music being played. So myself and a few others left and began putting together Alternative Broadcasting Cork (ABC Radio).

'The initial plan was to be an alternative to RTÉ Cork Local Radio, which at that time was broadcasting for just one hour per day, 12.30 p.m. to 1.30 p.m. We broadcast from 8 a.m. to 9 p.m., with a great line-up.'

'Ex-pirates like myself, John Creedon and Mark Cagney would go on to work for RTÉ and be recipients of Jacob's Radio Awards for our respective programmes.

'Pirate radio was all about the music, and developing the very best radio we could. We were always trying out new things. It was very much "backpack" radio. The studio was sparse, the equipment was basic, but it was not going to limit our great love for radio. We wanted to be professional in every way possible: coming in with prepared scripts, having well-researched guests and, most importantly, playing great music.

'We had fun; it was hilarious at times, really. I remember going in one day and finding a singer with his electric guitar plugged into the studio H&H amp, and going directly out on air. It's a wonder it didn't blow up on us.

'Sometimes the transmitter would go on the blink and so one of the jocks would go out to the kitchen area (that's where the transmitter was sitting) and hold a fluorescent tube up to it to check the signal strength. Get two jocks doing this and invariably a Star Wars light saber moment ensued.

'At one of our presenters' meetings it was suggested that at the weekends we should stay on air through the night. There were no objections and so the idea was launched with great enthusiasm.

'One night I was heading home at around 3 a.m. and turned on the car radio to listen to ABC. All I could hear was a clicking sound, so I drove to the studio at some speed to discover the jock head-down in front of the mic snoring away in deep sleep. The turntable needle had reached the last track on the LP.

'Every presenter had a radio name, if only to conceal his true identity; we were, after all, illegal. My mum had christened me Stephen Christopher after my grandfathers. I started out as Steve Christian but finally settled on Chris Stevens.

'My colleagues were opting for more colourful names that might have been best suited to a local hair salon or a newly opened boutique. Consequently we had jocks trading as John Patrick, Mark Anthony, Peter James, Mark Peters – you get the idea.

'After some months of really exciting radio we were the station of choice for listeners on Leeside. What could possibly go wrong?

'Again we got raided by the Department of Posts and Telegraphs, accompanied by members of An Garda Síochána. They removed all our transmission equipment. The ending of my pirate radio days was nigh.

'In early 1979, the word was out that the national broadcaster was preparing to launch a music channel to take on the many pirate stations that were now springing up in every county. The station was to be known as RTÉ Radio 2 with the catchphrase "Comin' atcha". Interested presenters were invited to apply for positions so we all decided to give it a try.

'Some weeks later I got a phone call to say I was on the team at Radio 2 (as it was originally known) which officially opened on 31 May 1979. My pirate days were certainly over now.

'Through it all we had so much fun. It was never about making money. Back then almost all the male jocks sported big moustaches, large-collar disco shirts, flared denim suits, boogie fever, platform shoes and big hair. My beloved 1600 E Ford Cortina was my pride and joy.

'Would I do it all again? Absolutely, in a heartbeat!'

CHAPTER SEVENTEEN

Romano Macari: 'My earliest memory of pirate radio in Cork was when we had Rocky's Restaurant in the city centre. We put a small transmitter in and we were broadcasting from the back of the restaurant for the customers.

'When you'd come in to Rocky's, you could leave a request. When they were in their car heading home we would play their request and thank them for coming in to Rocky's. It was known as Rocky FM.

'It was a bit of a novelty to hear a request from the restaurant you had just been to. I haven't heard of it since then – the only restaurant in the world that had its own radio station.

'It wasn't a question of me being drawn to radio. I was involved in the music business back in Dublin in the old days. We always worked hand in hand as regards entertainment. I was one of the first guys, along with a fella called Justin James, to have a mobile disco on the road. That is going back forty years or so now.

'What we used to do was to rent out parochial halls in different towns. We had a truck with a tail-lift and our mobile disco was called "Star Track". It was built like a space capsule and it had all kinds of things like robots, all done in a light wood. We used to go around the country doing mobile discos in towns that didn't have clubs.

'I was also involved with bands in the early days. I was born into the food business but I kinda went full circle. When we did Rocky FM and we had the radio station, we had a problem. There was a fire at Rocky's but we continued the radio station on the very top floor while the restaurant was being repaired.

'We had Pete O'Neill and Rob Allen involved and, of course, Trevor Welch. We were broadcasting from upstairs so Rocky FM wasn't really the name to continue with. After the fire, we changed the restaurant into a fast food outlet and so we were talking about the radio station and, after considering it with Pete O'Neill, we said why not take over the SouthCoast mantle? That's how it came about. It would have been about the early or mid 1980s.

'We saw the niche. Back in those times you had Ford, Dunlop and Pfizer. There were a lot of closures, job losses and a bit of a depression in Cork at that time. The unemployment rate was really high. I think it was running about twenty per cent or so in Cork. There were loads of people out of work.

'Radio, we felt, wasn't really doing a service for the people of Cork. It was more than just playing the hits of the day. We wanted to give people a voice. People could come on, have a chat, talk about what was going on in their community and in the city. Talk about their lives. That is how the live phone-in was born with SouthCoast.

'People would talk about everything. We played requests for them and it proved a really popular format. We did one for a trial run and I decided to host that show because it was my brainchild. It worked out OK. I started building up a bit of a following and it pretty much proved to be an instant success. It was a popular show and it ran from 10 p.m. until 2 a.m.

'I don't know about being the Barry White of Cork radio, or if women loved the voice. But I was well received and I had a good listenership. We were guaranteed phone calls every night. It wasn't a question of whether people would ring – it was always ringing.

'That was vey evident at Christmas, I think it was 1984 or 1985, when we put an appeal out for toys for needy children and we filled three vans. I will never forget the reaction to the appeal – we filled the entire foyer with toys. It was incredible.

'There were so many funny stories from that time. There was one about the unemployment situation. This guy comes on the air and says "Romano, boy, I got myself a job." One of the things I used to ask people was whether or not they were working. I had a lot of people who weren't working or who had lost their jobs. This guy comes on and says he had got a job. The obvious thing to ask him was what kind of job it was? I thought he was a bricklayer or a mechanic or a street cleaner or something. But then he told me he got a blow job – it was hilarious although I was completely stunned by it at the time.

'I think we tried to turn the negativity around the city into something positive. I gave out to one guy on air for being a lager lout. The amount of people that reacted to it was unbelievable. The number of people that rang up or wrote to me sympathising for getting a guy like that on air was astonishing. It actually turned into something very positive – it was the talk of the town. Everywhere I went people brought up what had happened. Even today in Marbella people come up to me and ask about it.

'But one of the most memorable things that ever happened to me on air was a person talking about suicide. A woman came on air and told me she had just overdosed. She was from the Togher area. What happened was that she had an only son. I cannot recall if the son got married or if a girl went to live with him. But there were three of them in the house and the woman was turned into what was effectively a house slave. The son's partner wouldn't work around the house and the mother felt she was basically looking after three of them. If she mentioned it to the son, he would give out to her.

'In the end, neither the son nor his partner were talking to the poor woman and she just didn't want to continue being the maid in her own house. She was a widow and she was so depressed she basically decided to take her own life.

'She took an overdose and she rang SouthCoast in what was basically a cry for help. She got through on air which was difficult enough because it was busy and not every caller managed to get through. We spoke to her live on air – I will never forget it. We stopped all the music, we kept her talking on air and eventually got an address from her and, on the other line, we rang the Gardaí and they were able to go with an ambulance to her house.

'She was still live on air when the Gardaí and the ambulance arrived at her house and took her away to hospital. She nearly died of an overdose. That was one of the greatest moments I think we ever had with SouthCoast because we definitely helped to save that poor woman's life.

'SouthCoast moved around Cork quite a bit. We were the very first pirate station in Ireland to have National Union of Journalist (NUJ) members. Before EastCoast Radio or anyone else, we had NUJ – registered people working with us with the union's approval.

'We moved to Togher and into the Pyramid snooker club. They were great days for us. There was so much fun and so many happy memories. We were treated really well there. One time we broadcast live for a twenty-four-hour snooker marathon. We even interviewed the Bishop of Cork at one point as part of it.

'One day we did three different outside broadcasts in a single day which was some undertaking for a pirate station. We did an outside broadcast on Patrick Street at the same time we had Neil Prendeville in Wimbledon in the box for the tennis final and we had another feed from New York where the Statue of Liberty was being uncovered following a major restoration programme.

'The whole thing was amazing – Cork was full of characters. It was a remarkable city to live in at the time. You had Bernie Murphy and people like him. But you also had the lads who cut their teeth in pirate radio who were suddenly making a name for themselves nationally. You had John Creedon who had only just moved up to the Big Smoke. There was Neil Prendeville, Paul Byrne, Trevor Welch, Mark Cagney, Ken Tobin and all the others.

'I suppose we didn't think anything was beyond us at the time. We did special live shows from places like the Lough Tavern and the Powdermills in Ballincollig. Sometimes, I would wear a tuxedo to the broadcast just to make a bit of fuss over it. It's hard to believe, looking back on it now, but people used to get buses out to the venue. It would be absolutely jammed for the live broadcast – maybe 300 or 400 people crammed into the pub. To be honest, I would arrive and think I was some kind of superstar.

'A woman one night came right up to where I was broadcasting, opened her shirt, took off her bra and revealed all to everyone around. I was a very shy lad and didn't know what to make of it.

'It was an amazing time in Cork because you had such great nightclubs as well. There was Cocos which was a great club and tied up with us a lot for broadcasts, particularly when we were based on Cook Street. Dominic O'Keeffe (DJ Domino),

God rest him, of the club was an amazing guy and he was such a sad loss.

'Dominic was larger than life. Dominic, myself and a guy called John Murphy – we were three buddies and all of our birthdays were within weeks of each other's so we would have one big bash every year in Cocos around 22 September. It was a night to remember for everyone.

'People forget but Cocos hosted the Liverpool football team when they played in Cork, Rory Gallagher would go in there – it was the happening place in Cork. There was something special about that time and lads from RTÉ used to call down to see me and would sit in our studios when we were broadcasting just to get a flavour of what we were at.

'Gerry Ryan called in to us one day. I think he was in town for an RTÉ "Beat on the Street" event but he wanted to see for himself what was happening with SouthCoast. Gerry had his roots in pirate radio in Dublin and I think he was very open to what was going on outside RTÉ. He was another tremendous loss. Such a terrible shame – a lovely guy and such a wonderful talent.

'Mark Cagney was another who was tuned in to what was happening with pirate radio around the country. He would also call in to see us and listen to what we were up to. Mark was a very smart guy and knew the business.

'Pirate radio gave me an amazing series of years. It was a magical time. You looked forward to the show every single night. It was never boring, you never dreaded the idea of going in to the studio. Every day that you went on air you were counting down the minutes to your show. Pirate radio gave me such a buzz.

'But it also left a sour taste in my mouth at the finish. Because, when the time came for the licenses to be handed out, we were getting an application together and we were approached by a certain group who said to us: "Why would we bother applying independently when we could all amalgamate?" I was invited on board and was told I would be a shareholder and would be guaranteed a show.

'I decided it sounded better that we put all our resources into the same hat. I spoke to a few people who were behind us and they said it would be the way to go because it would be very hard to beat them because they were the "Kings of Cork city". Basically, I said "OK, let's run with it." They were supposed to be drawing up a contract for me to sign but every time I asked about it I was told it would be ready the next week.

'One day I went to a meeting only to be told I wasn't welcome there anymore. What happened was they were happy for me not to make an application because they felt the popularity of SouthCoast in Cork might have been a threat to them. We had been working to get finances behind us but they got what they wanted in terms of distracting us. We had a very powerful Fianna Fáil businessman in Cork who was interested in financing us but, when I approached him about the amalgamated bid, he told us it was the way to go.

'We felt confident in the early days about our bid. Maybe that is why the rival group approached us even though most people reckoned they were already the frontrunners. We threw our lot in with them but what they did then was pull the wool over our eyes and stall us until the submission deadline was past and finally they told us to "fuck off".

'I always try to take people at face value and that did leave a sour taste in my mouth. I was so disappointed that I pretty much ended my involvement in radio after that. It was like a very happy part of my life had been taken away from me. I felt I had been a fool to allow myself to be taken in. I trust people – that is my nature. But I felt that I had been taken advantage of.

'If I'm honest, I don't think Radio South or 96FM filled the void that was there. What we created with SouthCoast was something really special and a lot of the credit for that has to go to Pete O'Neill. He was an amazing guy. No one ever brought back the magic we had on air. What took over was a far more profitable but highly commercialised product. I suppose it has to be but we had the magic – a family feel to the radio station that people responded to.

'The shows back then weren't planned and analysed. Every show was different – the DJs picked their own music, there were no playlists and shows weren't clones of each other. I left Cork in the early 1990s and went up to Dublin. I went back into the food business and I moved to Spain a few years ago. I have a business in Spain – I operate a music bar in Puerto Banus. We have a bit of karaoke and the like.'

Romano still retains strong links with Ireland and is a frequent visitor. Hardly surprisingly, entertainment runs deep in the Macari DNA and both his daughters have forged successful show business careers. Virginia starred in the TV series *Dublin Housewives* and also appeared on the *Podge & Rodge Show*. She has also worked as a successful model. Sonya is now an actress based in Hollywood, having trained at the Gaiety School in Dublin and later the Herbert Bergoff Studio in New York. She has appeared in TV series including *The Tudors, Glee, House, Chuck* and the science fiction film, *Protocol*.

CHAPTER EIGHTEEN
The End

In the end, it was the very success of the super pirates that brought about their own demise.

ERI and SouthCoast amply proved what the government should have realised years before – that commercial radio was a burgeoning source of tax revenue, not to mention badly needed employment. Just like Radio Nova and 98FM in Dublin, the Cork super pirates became slick, money-making machines. The smart pirates paid tax on all their earnings, garnering grudging respect from the Revenue Commissioners and Department of Finance officials looking to maximise every state income possible in the grip of a major recession.

RTÉ's powerful arguments against making the pirates legal began to be undermined by the clear recognition that here was a valuable source of funding for the state. Moreover, pirate stations had shown through their news and current affairs coverage that they could match, and in certain cases out-muscle, the national broadcaster in terms of local coverage, a fact not lost on the politicians who were often featured on the ERI and SouthCoast bulletins.

A media-savvy Cork politician who might be lucky to feature on RTÉ once or twice a month could be heard on SouthCoast or ERI every forty-eight hours. It was a lesson well noted by local councillors and shrewd TDs. Advertising revenue also began to soar on local radio as stations became more professional and businesses began to lose their fear of the consequences of advertising with pirates.

It was also now apparent that legalising the pirate stations would not trigger a doomsday scenario for either RTÉ or the print media. The success of the super pirates, coupled with the continued success of RTÉ and Ireland's national and provincial newspapers, meant that there was clearly enough advertising revenue in the market. Those who advocated against competition were quickly reminded that Ireland was an open market European economy.

Dublin TD Jim Mitchell (FG) had done more than anyone to help address the decade-old problem of precisely what to do with the pirates. But it was ultimately left to fellow Dublin TD Ray Burke (FF) to grasp the nettle under Charles Haughey's minority government from 1987–9. In December 1983, Mr Mitchell outlined the scale of the pirate radio problem to the Fine Gael-Labour coalition at a time when RTÉ was still pressing for the funding to be allowed to set up its own network of regional stations to combat the pirates at grassroots level.

'It is believed that there are at present about fifty illegal radio stations broadcasting in different places throughout the country. Many of them operate in the Very High Frequency Band (VHF) and a number of these stations appropriated frequencies in a part of that band which, under international agreement, is not available for use by broadcasting stations at present,' Mr Mitchell wrote.

'The present wave of illegal use of broadcasting equipment started in the mid 1970s. By about 1980, commercial interests became involved and it became clear that a determined effort was being made to establish commercial radio stations in open defiance of the law. By 1980/81 two powerful stations were set up in Dublin and these were quickly emulated in other parts of the country.'

Government crackdowns, including raids and seizures of equipment by the Gardaí, followed by court appearances and fines, successfully thwarted the development of stations. But it was a signal failure in terms of permanently wiping them out. Stations simply moved offices, bought new equipment or renamed themselves. Even substantially increased fines of up to IR£50,000 (€64,000) failed to deter the pirates who were now on the cusp of a wave of both advertising revenue and audience popularity.

Mr Mitchell also outlined the scale of the problems being caused by pirate radio stations as he argued for a legislative answer to the problem. 'Illegal radio stations have caused and continue to cause numerous problems and risks of unacceptable interference to authorized and licensed services both in this country and overseas.' The most famous consequence of the popularity of pirate stations was the collapse of part of the Dublin city telephone system in 1984 when a phone-in competition to a pirate station proved wildly popular.

Other problems weren't quite so light-hearted. Radio Sunshine was accused of interfering with the marine distress frequency used by shipping off Dublin; Radio Nova/KISS FM was found to have interfered with the Euronet communications network due to their 50kw transmitter which was more powerful than anything ever used by an Irish pirate station; Radio 257 was found to have interfered with the landing systems at Dublin Airport; Radio Metro had interfered with aircraft frequencies; several Cork stations were found to have interfered with radio systems at Cork Airport as well as, with less serious implications, interfering with the RTÉ TV signal for some homes around Cork.

Garda and emergency service radios regularly reported interference from pirate radio stations. In one famous incident, Cork Gardaí were receiving crystal clear music broadcasts over their handheld radios from a Cork pirate station. But the problem was also experienced by the fire brigade, civil defence and even the Defence Forces.

As early as 1983, Jim Mitchell was examining the potential for licensing the pirate stations while also increasing the fines and equipment seizures for pirates found to be making a nuisance of themselves. But, by 1983, it was also clear that a route would have to be found by government to allow the bigger pirate radio stations to operate legally – there was simply too much profit potential involved. By this time, serious business interests were also involved and they wanted the government to hammer out a legislative solution comparable to that which existed in the UK.

'Some illegal broadcasters have expressed interest in being licensed under the proposed local radio legislation. I would expect that, when the Local Radio Authority to be established under the new legislation is considering applications for franchises, it will have due regard to the behaviour of unlicensed operators who, despite repeated warnings, continue to interfere with vital services,' Mr Mitchell advised then-Taoiseach Dr Garret Fitzgerald in a private memo.

Critically, this became the kernel of the problem for the pirate stations in Cork – how to continue to operate and grow their audience without upsetting the authorities to the point where, when the long-awaited radio licenses were dished out, their application wasn't blackballed. It was a 'Catch 22' problem that would ultimately put paid to Cork's two dominant pirates, ERI and SouthCoast.

'Looking back it is hard to credit how the licence didn't go to either ERI or SouthCoast,' the late Cork North Central TD Liam Burke (FG) once admitted. 'They were both very strong and well-regarded stations but I think they both fell foul of problems which didn't hit pirate radio stations in other areas. If you look at Waterford, the licence there went to WLR FM which was effectively the consortium built around the old pirate station.' Liam Burke was well placed to know because ERI was based at White's Cross in his constituency.

The roll-out of the radio licenses was overseen by Communications Minister Ray Burke with the Dublin and Cork licenses amongst the most ferociously contested. The licensing process was overseen by the newly created Independent Radio and Television Commission (IRTC). However, the Cork licence was constructed in a format that took many by surprise. The city licence involved broadcasting rights to the city and its immediate environs with Cork county being catered for by two separate licenses. Shrewd analysts quickly realised that this could easily prove a poisoned chalice for the new city station with a substantial part of the existing pirate radio audience shorn away. It was also realised that a substantial part of the working population in Cork city and its environs lived in the county.

In the end, a total of twelve groups applied for four licenses set up to cover Cork city, city and county, and north Cork and Kerry (with parts of Cork county). There were three applicants for the city licence. The IRTC chairman, Mr Justice Seamas

Henchy, and IRTC secretary, Sean Connolly, ruled out any immediate changes to the franchise areas in Cork city and county following concerns on the part of one of the applicants that too many stations would be seeking advertising revenue in the city.

The writing was on the wall from an early stage for the former Cork pirates. Bids associated with ERI and SouthCoast came in for stiff questioning from Mr Justice Henchy during special oral hearings set up in Cork. Both Sound of the South and WKLR staunchly defended their positions during the bid hearings. However, both groups insisted that they would not accept any financial liability for debts associated with former pirate stations. In hindsight, it was a strategic mistake which would haunt both groups.

At the conclusion of the Cork hearings, Mr Connolly said the IRTC was required to look into the past history of applicants in echoes of what Mr Mitchell had said six years earlier. Ultimately, Sound of the South was forced to deny that it was merely a re-badged version of the old ERI station.

Mr Joe O'Connor, former chief executive of ERI and the largest shareholder of Sound of the South, told the IRTC the firms were separate, limited liability companies with no responsibility for each other. However, he admitted to Mr Justice Henchy that the Sound of the South would acquire some of ERI's assets if it was successful with its bid but would not be responsible for those pirate radio station's liabilities.

For some, the entire bidding process left a sour taste in the mouth. Romano Macari, who did much to make SouthCoast such a popular station in the mid 1980s, was so annoyed about how he was later treated that he left the radio industry altogether. 'It was like a very happy part of my life had been taken away from me. I felt that I had been a fool to allow myself to be taken in. I trust people – that is my nature. But I felt that I had been taken advantage of. I was so disappointed that I pretty much ended my involvement in radio after that,' he said.

The dark horse in the bidding process was the newly created Radio South. It was a bid fronted by respected journalists from *The Cork Examiner* with substantial backing from Cork business interests. The bid was fronted by *Cork Examiner* news editor Pat Casey, sports journalist Brendan Mooney and news reporters Peter Cluskey and Denis Reading. Critically, the bid didn't have any direct connection to the successful Cork pirate radio stations – something which proved both something of an immediate advantage and a long-term liability.

Radio South won the bid, much to the chagrin of Sound of the South, though a deal was quickly struck for the assets and valuable broadcasting equipment of ERI. The station went live on 10 August 1989 as the third of the newly licensed 'independents' to hit the airwaves, the other two both being in Dublin. The Lord Mayor of Cork, the late Councillor Chrissie Aherne (FF), was flown by helicopter to the station's interim White's Cross base and the first major programme was presented by Neil Prendeville. The first track played was Simply Red's 'A New Flame'.

Fans of the old Cork pirate radio stations found much of the new station comforting – as well as Neil Prendeville, there were familiar voices in Roger Ryan, Rob Allen, Tony Magnier and Joe O'Reilly. There was also excitement that, at long last, Cork finally had a commercial radio station of its own. But the honeymoon didn't last long and audience figures for early 1990 were disappointing. The station had been boosted by the arrival from *The Cork Examiner* of news reporter John Murray (who would go on to RTÉ fame) but programming and audience share issues continued unabated.

The station opted for a relaunch and a rebranding in July 1990 which delivered the 'Hits & Memories 96FM' banner. However, audience figures and revenues continued to fall below projected levels. The station suffered from the franchise's city broadcasting limitations and the fact it was not a clone of the old pirates and lacked their devil-may-care mystique. Radio South/96FM was a business and was expected to operate as such. By the time the station opted for a remodelling on the 'classic hits' system so favoured by Australian radio executives and used successfully by 98FM in Dublin, it was already too late.

'Radio South was a disaster from the point of view of programming or structure. You could hear anything at any time of the day,' Neil Prendeville recalled. 'It had no sense of familiarity when you turned the radio station on. It was a bit of a mess. It never had a hope and it wasn't long before it got gobbled up by bigger people with deeper pockets. The downside to it was that when radio stations change ownership, so many people get sacked. The whole station was virtually cleaned out overnight and some really good jocks lost their jobs. It was really terrible. The late, great Joe O'Reilly was literally scrapheaped overnight. It was all wrong.'

What was remarkable about Radio South was that it boasted such an enormous pool of talent – the very best journalists in Cork and the top presenters from the pirate radio era. It is worth noting that the station delivered two future RTÉ stars (John Murray and Peter Cluskey), a successful public relations executive (Pat Casey) as well as broadcasters of the calibre of Neil Prendeville, Paul Byrne and PJ Coogan, all of whom would carve out successful careers in Cork TV and radio. But, in hindsight, Radio South had simply been expected to deliver too much, too fast. Worst of all, it was simply unlucky.

In 1991, County Sound/103FM took over 96FM. Over the space of the next decade, the station came to dominate broadcasting in Cork and developed one of Ireland's biggest radio audiences. The station eventually saw off RTÉ Cork Local Radio and dominated the Cork scene until a second city station, RedFM, was licensed and began broadcasting in 2002. 96FM was further helped by a move from the old ERI base at White's Cross to Patrick's Place, just off St Patrick's Hill, where its headquarters overlooked the city centre. It was, as many of the 1980s pirate station executives had foreseen, a money-making machine.

County Sound ultimately sold control of the station to UTV who rigorously applied the 'playlist' model both to maximise commercial operations and to protect market share. In perhaps the ultimate irony, probably the most significant challenge 96FM has faced since then was the defection of former pirate radio star, Neil Prendeville, to RedFM in February 2014 and their newly relaunched morning chat show. The broadcaster brought his entire production team of Emer O'Hea-Martin and Colm Moore with him.

96FM immediately responded by handing the key morning talk show programme to former pirate DJ and award-winning radio journalist, PJ Coogan, with a new production team of Deirdre O'Shaughnessy and Brenda Dennehy. Coogan had filled in for Prendeville on various occasions and had proven both popular and successful. For arguably the first time in Cork licensed radio history, a serious ratings war was now underway with major advertising commitment from both stations in print, billboard and even cinema formats.

'Radio is big business these days,' TV3's Paul Byrne explained. 'It's all about market share, audience ratings and profitability. The romance of the old pirate stations is long gone. But you have to say that Irish commercial radio is amongst the most professional in the world. If you are trained on an Irish radio station you can walk into a station anywhere on the planet, get behind the mic and work. The standard is exceptionally high here.

'For my money, Ireland does "talk radio" about as well as anywhere in the world. There is none of the extremes you see in the United States – just really good content and an incredible bond with the local audience.'

The old pirates might not recognise the market studies, the high-tech equipment or the vast resources, but they would heartily approve of the professional standards achieved. In that regard, pirate radio has left arguably the greatest possible broadcast legacy in Cork.